Moving to My Dog's Hometown

"Through a series of interconnected flashbacks and stories, Vereckey discusses the unexpected twists and turns of her life, offering readers hope that healing and beauty can exist after a painful crossroads…This is a stirring account of one woman's quest to grow, gain insight, and heal from life's hurts."
—The BookLife Prize

"An honest portrait of someone trying to navigate through the unknown and figure out what home means when everything familiar has fallen away… Vereckey's engaging voice and warm observations keep the pages turning."
—*Kirkus Reviews*, a recommended pick

"Vereckey is a raconteur at the top of her game. This is a memoir that vividly evokes the power of community: how we find it; how we nurture it; how it shapes us."
—Ernest Scheyder, National Book Award-longlisted author of *The War Below*

"A funny, raw, and quietly luminous memoir…With sharp humor and deep tenderness, *Moving to My Dog's Hometown* proves that freedom isn't found in a perfect plan, but in the mess of beginning again."
—Kelly McMasters, author of *The Leaving Season*, a Good Morning America May Books Pick

"What I really love most about Betsy Vereckey's memoir is that it makes me believe in signs from the universe (even signs with fur and big noses) that can help guide us to a fresh start and find our way home."
—Joni B. Cole, author of *Party Like It's 2044*

"With equal parts candor and humor, Vereckey unleashes a page-turning tale about our very human need for companionship and a tender-hearted reminder that not all who wander are lost."
—Wendy Willis Baldwin, author of *The Sisters We Were*

"A love story of the best kind, *Moving to My Dog's Hometown* reminds us that with personal courage and meaningful support, we can endure life's toughest challenges…Vereckey shows resilience as she endures medical treatments for multiple sclerosis, forges new, nurturing ties with a chosen family, and adapts to stick season, snow, and foraging bears. For anyone stuck in a less-than-satisfying life situation, this is a story to inspire hope, for it assures us we can create happy next chapters."

—Marjorie Nelson Matthews, author of *The Red Wheelbarrow*

Moving to My Dog's Hometown

Stories of Everything I Didn't Know I Wanted

BETSY VERECKEY

Montpelier, VT

Moving to My Dog's Hometown: Stories of Everything I Didn't Know I Wanted
©2025 by Betsy Vereckey

Release Date: January 30, 2026

All Rights Reserved.
Printed in the USA.

Paperback ISBN: 978-1-57869-204-0

eBook ISBN: 978-1-57869-213-2

Library of Congress Control Number: 2025920023

Published by Rootstock Publishing
an imprint of Ziggy Media, LLC
Montpelier, VT 05602

info@rootstockpublishing.com
www.rootstockpublishing.com

Book design by Eddie Vincent, ENC Graphic Services.

Cover photo and author photo by Rob Strong, www.robstrong.com.

The stories in this book reflect the author's recollection of events. Some names, locations, and identifying characteristics have been changed to protect the privacy of those depicted. Dialogue has been re-created from memory.

No AI training. No part of this book may be reproduced or transmitted in any form or by any means, electronic or mechanical, including photocopying, recording, or by an information storage and retrieval system (except by a journalist or reviewer who may quote brief passages in an academic or editorial review) without permission in writing.

For reprint permissions, or to schedule a book club visit or author reading, contact Betsy through her website, www.betsyvereckey.com.

For Ronan and Jackie O.
And for anyone who has loved a dog with all their heart.

SEASON OF MY DISCONTENT

Canine Custody

My husband rolls up his sleeves, then folds his hands on the table. My husband. How many times I must have said that in my marriage, but after this meeting, I will no longer use those words because I will no longer have a husband.

Maybe I should have just gotten divorced on the Internet. My friend Eleanor left her husband with the help of LegalZoom, though it was apparently so complicated that half the time she wonders if she's even divorced.

My husband must want out of this soulless Manhattan conference room as much as I do, with its carpeted floors and fluorescent lighting. Outside, the world is carrying on as usual, people rushing to the subway or Macy's, just down the street. I wonder what kinds of terrible things have happened here. Do people ever throw chairs when they're getting divorced? Storm out? Surely, plenty of F-bombs have been dropped. Does being angry make divorce any easier? My marriage lasted only five years and feels like the end of a television series that's gone on past its prime.

Our mediator, Bonnie, shuffles a few papers across the table from us. She came recommended by a friend who said that her divorce was so easy it was like it never happened. That's exactly what I want. To pretend this whole thing never happened.

I'm dressed like a woman who looks like she has her life together—simple black dress, denim shirt, tote bag slung on the back of her chair—but I didn't have time to shower this morning because I overslept, thanks to the two NyQuil I took with a glass of wine last night to help me sleep.

"Becky, will you be hiring your own lawyer?" Bonnie asks.

Becky? "My name is Betsy. Actually, it's Elizabeth, for legal purposes. And no, I won't be hiring a lawyer. I think we can figure out everything today that we need to." My husband and I are still civil. We still text, sometimes even grab a drink. This should be fine, although it did feel awkward in the elevator ride up here together. Neither of us said a word.

Bonnie scribbles my name onto her legal pad, then places a hand on her belly. What are the odds? Of all the mediators in the world, we happen to get one who's pregnant. "Do you have any questions for me before we get started?"

Yes, I do, actually. How did I end up here, preparing to sign divorce papers? What did Bonnie do right that I didn't? If Jack and I had moved to England, back to his small hometown with just each other and a container of Marmite, maybe I'd be the one reading *What to Expect When You're Expecting*.

That was what I wanted, what I thought would happen after we got married. We'd start a new life together in England. I had wanted that ever since we started traveling to London to visit his friends and family at the start of our relationship. We were always on the first flight out: Virgin Atlantic flight 26, New York City to London. After a quick drive to a friend's flat, we'd toss our bags onto the bedroom floor, a small, damp room with loud, opinionated heaters. Jet-lagged, we held each other in a narrow bed with mismatched sheets. It was the happiest I could ever recall being in my marriage, in that tiny bed in a room with an empty closet and windows splattered with thick raindrops, looking out onto old Victorian row houses. I could've laid in that bed for the rest of my life.

Except, Jack didn't want to live in England ever again, in the same way that I never wanted to return to Ohio after my mother died when I was twenty years old. That was what brought us together. I never had to explain to him what it felt like to be part of a fractured family, but now I wonder if that was part of our problem. Can you have a successful marriage with two people who avoid conflict, who run from the past?

"So, no children?" Bonnie asks, looking over our paperwork.

"No," I say, before Jack has the chance.

Bonnie shuffles her papers. Oh, how I wish I could think of something from my marriage worth mediating, something to prove that it all wasn't a total waste. What have Jack and I accumulated as a married couple? Aside from two televisions, bar tabs, and an espresso machine—the most expensive item on our wedding registry and now broken.

"Any other shared property?" she asks. "Retirement benefits?"

Retirement. Old age.

I thought we were going to grow old together.

It's what Jack said the day we agreed to separate. I once wanted that. I was always able to see us at the end of our lives. The problem was that I couldn't see the in-between—how we'd get there, how time would pass, how we could both get what we wanted out of life. I wanted so badly to see the future. Were we going to turn a corner, and if so—when?

We tried everything to save our marriage, including therapy. After most sessions, we went to the bar to drink it all away. We were as indecisive about our marriage as we were about ordering takeout. Before we knew it, a couple of hours had passed and we hadn't decided on anything. How would we ever decide where to live or whether to have children if we couldn't decide between tofu pad Thai or veggie burgers?

In the end, we landed at different destinations, wanting different things, and now it is impossible for me to not think about the life I was meant to have every time I see a Virgin Atlantic airplane.

"Should we move on to timelines?" Bonnie asks.

A text message pops up on my phone, showing a photo of Ronan in the background. Ronan!

"You can mediate our dog!"

I spin my phone around to show Bonnie the photo: one giant close-up of Ronan's dark, wet nose.

"Is his head supposed to be that big?" she asks.

It is. Ronan is a Glen of Imaal terrier, a scruffy Irish breed that looks like the puppy that might have resulted from a threesome between a lion, a polar bear, and a seal.

Four years ago, Jack and I picked him up from Susan and Jake, a quirky middle-aged couple in Hanover, New Hampshire. I didn't really know the first thing about dogs. I had always been a cat person. We showed up at Susan and Jake's house with everything we thought we needed—a leash, dog toys, a crate—but didn't have the most important thing: a name. We wanted something Irish. I had been thinking about Jimmy or Seamus, but after meeting our puppy for the first time, I had to admit that he didn't seem like either.

"I quite like the name Ronan," Jack said. It was summer then. We were sitting in the backyard, going over some last-minute grooming instructions from Susan.

"His dad was named Ronan too," Susan said. "My nickname for him is Trouble. He knocked down a lamp just before you got here."

Maybe that should've been red flag number one, that our puppy's name was Trouble. But then the next morning before we left town, we found a valet ticket on the ground in our hotel's parking garage. The name *Ronan* was on that ticket. It seemed too perfect to be a coincidence.

Just the thought of him at home in my apartment relaxes me. He's probably sprawled out on the couch in one of his acrobatic sleeping positions, his big, white fluffy head dangling off an armrest, two floppy ears covering his eyes. Later tonight when I walk in the door, he'll thump his tail against the cushion, completely clueless that earlier today his mom and dad called it quits.

I had hoped a dog would give Jack and I more opportunities to be together, but it actually did the opposite. Jack walked Ronan in the morning, and I took him out in the evening. I dropped Ronan off at the groomer's. Jack picked him up. The fantasy I had of walks every weekend morning along the East River with the three of us was squashed by Jack's soccer games on the television, his escape for long hours at the office. By the end of our marriage, I was the one who took Ronan on loops around the neighborhood, past the New York Stock Exchange and down to Battery Park, where Ronan would sit on a park bench with me, watching the ferries coming from the Statue of Liberty. On the way home, we stopped at Leo's Bagels, right around the corner from our apartment. Jack wasn't a big bagel person (that should've been red flag number two), but I liked to cap off the walk with an egg-and-cheese sandwich.

"Have you decided who will get custody of Ronan?" Bonnie asks.

Easy answer. "Me." Jack travels a lot for work. It makes more sense for him to be with me.

"What about joint custody?" Bonnie asks.

Joint custody. I probably should have offered that. God, how do people do this with actual kids and not dog children? I guess I could share Ronan as long as I get the important holidays. I need to be able to put shamrocks on his head to celebrate St. Patrick's Day and his Irish heritage. And during Christmas, I need to be able to walk Ronan past the pine trees on the sidewalks so that he can lift a leg on them.

I can't lose Ronan. Today, I am saying good-bye to my husband forever. I have prepared myself for that. But if I lose Ronan, I have nothing.

"Maybe I could take Ronan during the week, and you could have him on the weekends?" I ask. "I could bring him over from Brooklyn in a taxi..."

"No, no," Jack says. "You take him."

I feel a familiar urge to take Jack's hand, but that defeats the whole point of why we're here in this conference room. Divorce is always a possibility when you get married, but you never think it'll happen to you.

"Are you sure?" I ask.

He nods. "Ronan belongs with you."

It's true. Ronan might have been Jack's idea, but he's been mine ever since the beginning. I don't know where I'd be without him. All those mornings when I was so depressed that I couldn't get out of bed, Ronan sprawled himself out on top of me and placed his wet nose inches from mine, panting on me with his doggie morning breath, begging for a walk.

Bonnie scribbles down a few notes and clicks her pen. "I'll start drawing up the papers."

I glance at the time. You can't rush the future, but the past is a different story. Five years of marriage, gone in an hour.

Maybe You're Being Led

I cross my legs and lean back on my therapist's couch. There are several chairs in Joy's office, but I always sit in this one. It has the best view of Manhattan in the evening when the sun sets and casts a golden glow on the rooftops. Her office is right down the street from my office, where I work as a copywriter at an agency.

"Do you want me to get out my deck of oracle cards?" Joy asks, tying her long gray hair back in a low ponytail.

I feel lucky that I have Joy, who is as woo-woo as I am, the type of therapist who doesn't flinch when I blame my current circumstances on Mercury retrograde. I should be spending our hour together talking about my divorce, but today we're tackling an even bigger problem. My new apartment is infested with mice, a New Yorker's most common nightmare. They are truly everywhere: in my closet, in my living room, even my oven. I see them so often that when I'm out in the world, I've started to confuse inanimate objects for mice: empty water bottles rolling back and forth on buses, leaves rustling on the sidewalk. What oracle card is good for dealing with this kind of insanity?

"Why am I doing this? Going into debt for an apartment overrun with mice?"

"Let's try and reframe this," she says.

I don't know if Joy will understand. She's a lifelong New Yorker, born in Queens, with a rent-controlled apartment in the Village. "There's nothing to reframe. It feels like the mice are forcing me out of my apartment."

"Maybe you're being led."

Being led. I like that. But to where? It would be far more helpful if I knew where I was supposed to be going, other than out of my mind.

"Would you like to borrow my cat?" she asks.

I barely remember what it was like to be a cat person. I wish I could take Joy up on it, but I don't know how well cats get along with terriers, especially one who's an only child. "Thanks, but Ronan might not like that."

We don't make much headway on my mouse problem, but that's okay because I arrive home to find a present outside my apartment door: a pile of mousetrap boxes from the landlord. There's a tiny cartoon mouse on the cover with a pear-shaped body and pink ears, unaware of his fate. *Nontoxic*, the box says. How can the traps be nontoxic if they kill mice?

I'm not ready to murder anything. After eleven years in New York City, I'm still thinking of my mice the way I do all my old roommates who never did the dishes, never bought toilet paper, and never apologized for stealing my clothes and sleeping with their boyfriends in my bed. Annoying? Absolutely. But not quite worthy of the death penalty.

I think what really bothers me about the mice is the unexpectedness of it all. It's all very disgusting, don't get me wrong, but it would bother me less if I knew when and where the mice planned to appear. Maybe then we could just avoid each other?

I can't fathom moving again until one night a few weeks later when the mice are bold enough to scurry into my bedroom. I jump onto my bed. Ronan comes bounding in a few moments later. "Go get them! You're a terrier for God's sake!" Serves me right for raising him metrosexual. He crawls on top of me and starts panting, the way he does during thunderstorms. I send out a few S.O.S. texts. One of them is to Jack. He responds right away.

Fuck's sake! Go to my apartment. I'm in London. Stay as long as you need to. I'll put your name on the list with the doorman.

By "my apartment," he means our old apartment, a landmine of memories, where we cuddled next to each other on an air mattress our first night in the place, the one where we started our life together as a married couple. Do I really want to go back there? Would I rather spend the night in an apartment that's infested with mice or one that's busting at the seams with sad memories? I moved across the East River specifically so I wouldn't have to be reminded of the life I left behind, but I have nowhere else to go tonight. It's raining. It's late. A hotel will set me back several hundred bucks. Having Ronan makes it a lot harder to crash on someone's couch, especially if that someone has cats, like my friend Eleanor. Or has babies or lives somewhere where dogs are not allowed. Or even worse, does not like dogs.

Maybe I should double my NyQuil dose and just stay here. But what if a mouse crawls into my mouth when I'm sleeping? I stuff a duffel bag with spare clothes, then hail a taxi in the rain. I'm so relieved when a driver finally stops that I slide my wet fingers through the glass partition and tip him before we've even started driving.

One very awkward conversation with the doorman later, I ride the elevator up to the nineteenth floor. What a hassle this was when I had to potty-train Ronan. I had to hold him so he wouldn't pee on the floor. Now he's a big boy sitting at my side, wagging his tail because he thinks life has gone back to normal. I drop the leash and let him run down the hallway. Sure enough, he remembers where we're going and stops right at the door like old times. I turn the doorknob. The door slams shut behind me. I scan the room. The last time I was in this apartment was the day I left. I had the movers come when Jack was at work, thinking it would be easier on both of us if they didn't move me out when he was here, but now that seems pointless because I've somehow found my way back.

The ceilings are the same height but feel much lower. The chew marks on the legs of the coffee table are still there from when Ronan was a puppy. Same carpet, same pee stains. I raise the blinds on the windows, but like always, my only view is of the neighboring apartment. There used to be a woman who walked around naked, but she isn't there today. The only thing that looks new is a giant plant in the corner. Was it a suggestion from one of his friends? *Get a plant, mate. It'll help.*

Ronan jumps onto the couch and props a paw on the armrest. I plop down beside him. I had wanted a big couch, one that Jack and I could both lie on comfortably, and as a result, this brown leather one we decided on ended up being an inch too big for the service elevator.

In hindsight, we should've taken measurements and planned better, but when we saw the couch, we knew we didn't want anything else. We contacted a company called the Sofa Surgeons, who sliced the leather couch into two pieces, then put them back together. You'd never know looking at the couch what had happened to it. It felt like such a win at the time, fixing that problem, but all I can think of now is how far away Jack seemed at the other end.

We did the same thing with the television, bought one that was way too big. It's off now, but I bet it's tuned to the soccer channel. In Jack's younger days, long enough ago that he still had hair, he played semi-pro soccer. The World Cup was on the year we got together, and we had a fun time sidling up at the bar to watch, but I couldn't deal with a Wayne Rooney penalty kick before I even had the chance to have coffee.

To escape soccer on the weekends I took Ronan out for a pee, while Jack stayed put on the sofa, dressed in a hoodie and gym shorts with the insignia of his favorite soccer team, the Tottenham Hotspurs. I'd return to find him dashing out from the bathroom to check the score in the middle of trimming his beard, electric razor in hand, the same one I used to shave his head when we first started dating. I loved doing that for him. It felt so intimate, running my hands over his bald head. That all stopped when Jack started going to the barber.

I wander into our bedroom, where there's another large television dangling on the wall. I didn't like having so many televisions in the apartment, but it seemed like I argued more with myself than with Jack. Was it really a big deal if he wanted to watch television every morning? Soccer was his lifeline back to England, his fun for working long hours at the office. How could I ask him to turn it off? Now, I wish I had. If only we hadn't installed those televisions. Where might our relationship be then?

I unzip my duffel bag and start to hunt around for my pajamas when the silver ring holder catches my eye. It's two-pronged, shaped like an X. Eleanor had bought it for Jack as a joke, and I can't believe it's still out, on a bedside table. He had a bad habit of taking off his wedding ring, then forgetting where it was.

One day, toward the end of our marriage, Jack came home and paced back and forth in the living room, rubbing his head, the way he did when he was nervous and watching a soccer game. He was so distraught. I actually thought he was going to tell me someone had died.

"I lost my ring," he said.

He paid extra for a comfort fit. It seemed like a good investment, given that when you buy a wedding ring, you assume you'll be wearing it for a lifetime. But maybe a ring shouldn't be as comfortable as sweatpants or a couch. Maybe a marriage shouldn't be either. If it is, you get lazy. And, eventually, you stop noticing each other.

Jack felt terrible about losing the ring, but I felt even worse. Several days had passed, and I hadn't even noticed he was no longer wearing it. We looked everywhere, but it never turned up.

Now, Ronan jumps up on the bed next to me with an old dog toy he's found from who knows where. At least one of us is fine being back here.

"Did you eat the ring?"

He rolls onto his back and sighs. Guess I'll never know.

The Black Cloud

A woman behind the glass counter glances at the Polaroid in my hand. "How much sleep are you getting?"

My first aura reading isn't off to a great start.

"Eight hours," I say, though I'm not sure how that's relevant, and I don't mention the NyQuil. I probably wouldn't even need it if I didn't have several lattes a day at the coffee shop around the corner from my office, but the escape is well worth it.

My friends and I have come to Chinatown to get our auras read, and there's a long line outside the door. We're all pretty miserable at work, and we're hoping that we'll be able to glean some meaning from aura photos that are supposed to measure the electromagnetic fields around our bodies and translate them into colors. All of this is to say, we're feeling pretty desperate, but this is the kind of thing we do when we need guidance from the cosmos. We've been calling ourselves the Moon Squad ever since we went to a full moon ceremony in Brooklyn one Sunday afternoon. We're always looking for witchy things to do around New York City. We've made wishes on magical candles in the East Village and gone crystal shopping in Chelsea. My work friends are, without a doubt, the best part of my job.

I want my aura photo to look like me, but it doesn't feel recognizable. My body is barely visible in the picture. Maybe the woman behind the counter senses my disappointment. She points to a smudge of magenta and tells me that I'm creative.

This is what we're called in advertising—creatives—but as a copywriter who spends her day as a ghostwriter mimicking other people's voices, I wouldn't call myself that. Every day, I take a painfully slow elevator up a dozen flights to my office to the land of soulless work, where I spend my entire day trying to sound like someone else. Not even the view of Manhattan, high up on our office roof with teapot-shaped water towers, helps. People in neighboring glass skyscrapers peering out of their windows must think my coworkers and I are living the dream on the roof of our building, sprawled out on poppy-hued cushioned benches with our laptops. But what the white umbrellas and lush green plants hide are the mind-numbing ads and slogans on our computer screens that we've designed for real estate and insurance companies.

To make it more manageable, I go by Kim at work. It's my alias, an idea given to me by my boss, no less, to make what I'm doing more tolerable. Kim. One syllable, no complications. Kim can handle terrible client criticism. She's a good enough writer that she can make even insurance sound interesting. She gets the job done, and that's enough for her.

Then, there's Betsy. She yearns for more creative work. She can't imagine herself in this job five years from now, or a year from now for that matter. She often looks around her open office and wonders if anyone else feels the same way. If so, why isn't anyone saying anything?

How come I'm not saying anything? Because I'm scared I'll make another wrong choice, like I did by getting married?

Annie waves her aura photo back and forth. "This is so much better than being at the office."

"Being at the gyno is better than being at the office," says Sarah, a confident, Beyoncé-loving Virgo with a tell-it-like-it-is personality. I'm not surprised that in her pink-and-green photo, she's front and center, completely visible.

"What does the green mean?" I ask.

"Money. Maybe I'm going to get that raise after all."

Bridget scoffs. "When hell freezes over."

I know by now that money isn't everything. I gave up my job as a reporter several years ago, even though the newsroom felt like home to me. It was the perfect job to have when I first moved to New York City. I cared about my job so much I would often go home and think about how I could have written a story better. The drawback was the pay. As my twenties wore on, I began to want an apartment of my own, without roommates, and to do that in New York City, I needed a higher-paying job. So, I left. I gave up on my dream of living abroad as a foreign correspondent. I make more money now, and I can afford to live alone, but is it worth it?

Annie twiddles her pink aura photo in her hand. She's the youngest one out of all of us and a Gemini, like me. I can't keep up with all the women she's dating right now. Every morning when we meet in our favorite coffee shop before work, she walks in with a disheveled pixie haircut, and I know she's been up to no good but in the best way possible.

And, of course, there's Bridget, who's even more miserable than I am. She and I sneak out for lattes every chance we get. Her aura photo is splattered in crimson, fitting for a fiery Scorpio who never leaves the house without donning black eyeliner, whereas I barely wear makeup anymore.

"Do you have any questions about your photo?" the woman behind the counter asks me.

"Can you tell me what my future holds?"

That's what I really want to know. I have been obsessed with predicting the future ever since my mother and I started reading our horoscopes together. I never understood how several sentences could apply to a group of people united only by the month and day they were born, but my mother, an intuitive Pisces, encouraged me to look a little deeper. If it was a good horoscope, she'd cut it out of the newspaper and tape it to a greeting card and send it off to me when I was in college. Her cards usually arrived after the date in question, but that was never the point. *What does it mean to you?* she'd ask. She would love it here, where they tell you what kind of crystal you should get based on your astrological sign. Sometimes I read the horoscope for Pisces just to bring me a little closer to her. She died when I was in college. Since then, I've learned how to interpret an astrology chart, and one of the first things I do in the morning is check what the planets are doing, the way normal people check the weather forecast. I know you can't predict the future, but that doesn't ever stop me from reading my horoscope.

The woman behind the counter points to a burst of purple on the bottom right-hand side of my photo. "Happiness is on the way."

Finally, some good news.

"But first, you have to deal with this." She points to an ominous dark cloud over my head.

Great. My aura is black. Makes sense. Guess I'll just tuck this photo away in my closet with my wedding album. Maybe I should just burn it. Is this the vibe I'm giving off? Black-aura girl?

What I want is a pretty aura, bubbles of happy colors, but I guess that wouldn't be true. When I look in the mirror now, all I notice is a small line the length of a fingernail by my right eyebrow. I call it my divorce wrinkle because it didn't appear until recently. I've been in denial about aging, in the same way I never thought my marriage would fail. But now there's proof: my first wrinkle, a permanent reminder of what happened. At least my glasses sort of hide it.

Maybe I should get Botox. Or try to redo my aura photo. Or change my life. Get a new job? Move somewhere else? Would that make a difference? At the very least, I need to stop making my divorce-wrinkle face.

"There's too much going on in your mind," the woman says. "Have you tried meditation?"

Meditation? I do not want to sit with my dark thoughts. I know what my mother would tell me to do. She'd say, "Do what makes you happy." The problem is, I don't know what that is anymore.

Annie lines our Polaroids side by side on the glass countertop. It's striking to see all four of them next to each other. They feel accurate, as different as the four of us. Bridget's red photo, Annie's pink one. Sarah's rainbow and my Debbie Downer. I can't believe I didn't notice the dark cloud at first. Now I see nothing else.

Scrambled Eggs

With my legs in two stirrups, I hold my breath as a doctor sticks an ultrasound wand into my vagina to say hello to my ovaries. I have a hunch that freezing my eggs isn't going to be easy. Every few minutes, I sneak a glance at my doctor's face. There is something about him I do not care for, but it is hard to know if what I don't like is that I am paying him to get involved in my vagina because no one else has.

"If you tilt your head to look at the screen, we'll take a look at your left ovary."

The paper on the table crinkles. The top right corner of the monitor catches my eye.

"See?"

"Yes," I lie.

My doctor's voice is monotonous, suitable for narrating a documentary. He goes on and on about hormone injections, the blood tests I'll need to do every other day. How I'll need anesthesia when they do the egg retrieval. It all sounds pretty complicated, but there's really only one rule I need to know. Timing is everything.

I first started thinking about egg-freezing a few months ago when I was having dinner at an Italian restaurant. At the table next to me, two women my age were discussing it. By the end of the night, without even knowing it, they had convinced me to try it out, an eavesdropping stranger worried about her future. Who knows when I'll meet the next Mr. Right? Or what will happen if Mr. Right turns out to be Mr. Wrong again? Even if I met someone today, I'd need more time before dropping the "Hey, wanna have a baby?" conversation. Egg-freezing is my way of making up for lost time, for all the decisions I made when I was married that had seemed right at the time but now, in retrospect, were not so right after all.

I had always wanted to know what it would feel like to really want children, the way my mother did. She had two terrible pregnancies. When she gave birth to my older sister, the umbilical cord got caught around my sister's neck in utero, leaving her with developmental disabilities. Then when my mother was pregnant with me, she was diagnosed with German measles. Doctors tried to get her to have an abortion, convinced that I would be blind or deaf. My mother wouldn't hear of it. She always told this story with such conviction, but I often wonder what she thought about it all before she knew how things turned out, when I was still inside of her—what it felt like to take a chance like that, when the outcome was so uncertain.

I'm now the age she was when she had me—thirty-six—and I can't stop thinking that I'm behind schedule. The ideal time to freeze your eggs is when you are young, when your eggs are as ripe as an avocado that puckers with the light touch of a finger. But usually this isn't a time when you want to freeze your eggs because you still believe that life will work out on your own terms. If I had frozen my eggs a decade ago when I was in my twenties, I could have produced thirty-some eggs with little effort, but a decade ago I had just moved to New York City and was more concerned with finding the cool speakeasy hidden in an alleyway, the one with $13 cocktails served in porcelain teacups.

I was also dealing with a major health crisis. Not long after taking a job as a journalist, I started getting terrible headaches behind my right eye. I assumed it was just eye strain from working long hours, but when I went to the eye doctor to have it looked at, he realized that my optic nerve was inflamed, which had caused temporary vision loss. After an MRI, a spinal tap, and a few other tests, I was diagnosed with relapsing-remitting multiple sclerosis. Medication could help control the disease but wouldn't cure it. Ever since, I've known what it's like to live in an uncertain world. You could be on your way to what you think is going to be a routine appointment, and before you know it, you're in a taxi heading to the hospital. It made no sense. My mother didn't have MS. Neither does my father.

I was twenty-six when I was diagnosed. I had friends who were getting married and having babies, but children were the last thing on my mind. I couldn't grasp the idea of bringing life into the world when I worried that I would end up disabled one day.

After my appointment with the fertility doctor, I zip up my jeans, toss my gown in the bin, and hand over my credit card to the receptionist. My father has agreed to help me cover the cost, and I'm eternally grateful to him. We aren't super close like I was with my mother, but this is how he shows up for me: with money. My father doesn't know the ins and outs of egg-freezing, but he loves to gamble on the ponies, and in essence, that's what this is, one giant bet on my future. In my childhood, he covered the kitchen table with his horseracing forms, sketching out the odds of each horse with pencil marks. I used to think it was strange, until I realized I do the same thing with my astrological calendars. We both try to predict the future in our own ways.

He mails me a good old-fashioned check and tells me to keep him posted. By some cosmic synchronicity, I begin taking the medications on his birthday. This feels like a good sign, given that my father loves to pick lottery numbers and horses based on the time I was born.

Nothing about my life really changes at first. I meet the Moon Squad for happy hour at The Smith, our favorite local bistro, and assure them I am in no way hormonal as I cry while stuffing French fries into my mouth. I show up to work and get berated by clients. No one thinks I'm pregnant and offers me a seat on the subway, but when I walk around Manhattan, I feel different. Inside, I have a secret: I am growing eggs! Or at least I hope I am when I check in for my next appointment.

"So, how many eggs do you see in there?" I ask the doctor.

"It's hard to tell," he says, poking around with his ultrasound wand. "I see two follicles, maybe three."

"That's it?"

It's starting to feel like I'm on the wrong side of a very expensive bet. My ovaries are working overtime, but I am still not hitting double-digit egg production.

The doctor slides the wand around, and for the first time it feels a little familiar, like the terrible sex I used to have all the time in my twenties. "It is possible . . ." he says, while taking out the wand, "that there are more inside that the scan isn't picking up. It's still early. Let's see what happens." He snaps the white plastic gloves off his fingers. "Just remember we're fighting an uphill battle."

An uphill battle? If this were any other doctor's appointment, I'd grab my purse and head for the door and tell him where to put his uphill battle, but it feels like I'm already on a plane heading for I don't know where, and I can't get off until it lands. If I dump him, I'm out an obscene amount of money.

On my way out of the office, I pass a woman my age in the waiting room holding a stuffed animal. Why hadn't I thought to bring Mr. Bear?

Before going to work, I have my blood drawn at the fertility center a few times a week, my stomach becoming more bloated each day.

"If you're having sex, wear protection," the nurse warns.

If I were having sex, I wouldn't be in this predicament! A little flattered, I toss my hair and wonder if the hormones are giving me a boost. They're already affecting my appetite. I feel I have every right to eat anything that comes with ranch dressing, melted cheese, or a pickle on the side. *The kids need their nutrition.* Of course, I'll have an appetizer, an entrée, and a dessert, and no—are you crazy?—I will not share. No coffee after 4 p.m.! *The kids need their sleep.*

"Have you picked up any more?" Eleanor asks one night out at dinner, as if my eggs are Instagram followers.

I'm nearing the end of my hormone treatments, and we've met up for Italian in the West Village to celebrate however many sort-of children I have inside me. "Imagine if I got a whole dozen!" I say, leaning across the table. "But who knows? It's hard to say what's in there." I want certainty more than anything, but I just need to be patient.

Waiters pop champagne corks out of bottles. Chairs scratch across the wooden floor. With such low, cozy ceilings, it's always loud in Morandi. If I ever have children one day, are fun nights like this gone forever? Who knows, but it's fun to fantasize about the mother I might become.

Eleanor folds her napkin across her lap. "This is fascinating. I'm getting so attached to them."

So am I. The follicles might have been just little images on a monitor, practically invisible to the human eye, but I've started to imagine life growing inside me, even though I'm not sure whether what I'm actually looking at during my appointments is a spot of dust on the screen.

Halfway through the meal, Eleanor's boss, who's joined us for dinner, accidentally spills red wine all over the table, onto my purse, and into my lap. Ordinarily, I never like to see wine, especially Italian wine, go to waste, but it really seems like no big deal after everything I've been through this week. "Accidents happen," I say, sopping up the wine with our napkins.

A woman at the table next to us leans in close to me. "You were so calm when she spilled that wine. You must be a mother."

Eleanor and I exchange knowing glances. It's the first time anyone has ever called me a mother. I don't shudder away from it. Quite the opposite. I welcome it, the way I lean in toward the bread basket when I see our waiter approaching with our entrées.

The doctor estimates that the baker's dozen inside me will finish cooking on Sunday morning when the rest of Manhattan is at brunch having eggs over easy. I'm glad because by the end of ten days, I'm more bloated than a Macy's Thanksgiving Day balloon. I can no longer button my jeans on the day of the retrieval when I check in for my procedure with Eleanor, who hands me a good luck gift: a plastic egg full of candy.

"I'll be here when you get out."

An anesthesiologist leads me into the procedure room and gives me something to relax, which is a whole lot better than the NyQuil I've been taking.

This whole week, I've been thinking of how brave my mother was to go through with her pregnancy with me, after what happened to my sister. How scared she must have been to try for a second child when it went so terribly the first time. And then, somehow, a miracle. I came into the world on the eve of a full moon, perfectly fine. The bet she took on me paid off big time, a story she loved to tell to anyone who would listen. I wish I could see my future, how this will all work out. How many eggs will I have, and will I ever use them one day? Will this be the story I tell my children? No matter what, at least I can say I tried.

An hour later, I wake up to a foggy outline of a nurse with only one question on my mind.

"How many eggs did I have?"

She glances at my chart. "We got seven."

Lucky number seven! I knew I wasn't ever going to get into the double digits, but seven chances are better than nothing. The only thing that would make this better is getting to spend the rest of the day recovering on the couch with Ronan. I change into my jeans and take a taxi back to Brooklyn, where I order two pizzas to celebrate and spend the rest of the day lying down with my really good boy, watching the planes from my window, their arrival and departure times perfectly choreographed. I feel relieved that the experience is over, that I've done something to give myself a little more time to figure out my life.

The next day, I arrive at work in a good mood, even though it's a Monday morning. I have eggs on ice, seven chances at a future I didn't have two weeks ago. I sit down at my desk and open my email. It's early, but there's already a message from the fertility center. The doctor wants to talk. This doesn't sound good.

I walk into a conference room and dial the fertility center. He gets right to it. None of my eggs are great. Three of them were absolutely no good. They didn't have enough time to mature and had to be thrown out. As for the other four, they were slightly better, more mature but still not fully developed.

"Fragile," he says.

I can't think of a better word to describe the state I'm in right now. How did this all go so wrong? I stuck to their schedule and did everything I was supposed to do. My doctor encourages me to try again, proposing two alternatives for the next round (the next round?) of egg-freezing. One: Stay on hormones for longer than ten days to give the eggs more time to mature. Two: Try again with different medications. I don't know if I'll ever have kids, but I know one thing for sure. I'm never freezing my eggs again. If $10,000 can't buy you the perfect timing, then maybe nothing can.

Recalculating

A friendly sign inside my rental car reminds me that I have one responsibility and one only in Ireland—to drive on the left-hand side of the road. The message is in all caps for emphasis, just like the surgeon general's warning on a pack of cigarettes that basically says: THIS WILL KILL YOU.

Eleanor turns on the GPS machine after hopelessly fiddling with it like a Rubik's Cube. If I'm still so jet-lagged from my flight from New York that I don't remember where my passport is, how can I drive a moving vehicle where the steering wheel is on the wrong side of the car?

I pull out onto a narrow road and head west, toward Galway. Drive on the left ... drive on the left ... the car veers to the right. I can't seem to get the hang of this. Do I stay in the left lane when I turn? Or the right? It feels as if I'm driving a hearse disguised as a four-door sedan. "I don't think I can do this."

"You have to," Eleanor replies from the passenger seat, a scarf wrapped snugly around her neck. "It's your turn. I've already done the first leg."

This road trip along Ireland's Wild Atlantic Way seemed like a much better idea when Eleanor and I were still back in New York. Ireland has always been one of those countries that's on my airfare alert, a country that I will go to even if I'm so broke that I have to fly the plane myself. It's the perfect place to mourn my failed marriage and drink and cry at all hours of the day in dark pubs next to hot Irishmen.

As New Yorkers who don't own cars, Eleanor and I don't have much recent experience driving, let alone experience navigating the other side of the road, but at least if I die here, I won't have to go back home and deal with picky advertising clients and a mice-infested apartment.

A car honks. I swerve back into the left lane. The GPS falls off the dashboard and rolls onto the floor. Even with the warning sign directly in my face, I've already forgotten how to drive. Eleanor shoots me a look, the same one she's given me for the last twenty-five years whenever I've done something stupid, like when I had the idea to wax my own eyebrows in high school and ended up burning my skin.

I squint at the dashboard. It doesn't matter that we are in a country where English is the main language. Everything is foreign, including the speed limit on the GPS flashing in kilometers. I have no idea how fast we are driving in miles, but that doesn't matter because we have more pressing matters to attend to, such as staying away from other cars. Maybe we'll get picked up by a policeman for speeding. At least that would keep us alive a little longer. And maybe he'll be hot.

"Do you think the left lane is for slower traffic, like the right lane is back home?" Eleanor asks as we make our way onto the highway.

I don't know. I'm too busy making sure I'm still breathing. I know Eleanor is wondering if she should just take over, but this would mean she'd have to drive. She checks her phone, perhaps sending a goodbye text to her boyfriend, while I try to figure out how I'm going to get us through the roundabout up ahead. I miss the exit. The GPS flashes.

"Recalculating," a female voice says in an Irish accent.

I obey our new route and swing us back around. This time, I count the exits under my breath but still miss the road we are supposed to take. Another car sounds its horn.

"Sorry!" I yell.

"Recalculating," the GPS says.

"Why can't she get us back on track with a little encouragement?" I ask. "Something like, 'You're doing great! Make your next left. There's actually a nice pub close by with live music. Sounds like you might need a Guinness. Sláinte!'"

Eleanor closes her eyes and leans her head against the window. "I'm going to have vodka tonight."

Aside from the whole driving-on-the-wrong-side-of-the-road thing, being in the car with Eleanor feels like we're back in high school. Our conversations hopscotch between the present and the nineties, when we were teenagers who knew every showtune by heart, watched *Titanic* hundreds of times, and made shrines to Leonardo DiCaprio in our lockers. Back then, we never imagined we'd actually ever fall in love for real and get married, and we surely never imagined we'd be lost in Ireland trying to figure out what to do with our lives. I don't even know what to do with my engagement ring. For the time being, it's collecting dust in my jewelry box. One of my friends sold hers online; another suggested I give my ring to the future daughter I don't even know I'll have. Even so, I can't bear the thought of selling mine. It reminds me of when my relationship with Jack was good, when I still felt hopeful about love and marriage.

"Sheep!" Eleanor yells.

I slam on the brakes. A few of the sheep slowly turn in my direction.

"Jesus Christ, that was a close one," Eleanor says.

The sheep are everywhere, as ubiquitous as pubs and impossible to spot, despite the fluorescent streaks on their trunks. They travel in packs and take their time wandering across the narrow roads, blissfully unaware that two American divorcées are jet-lagged and headed straight for them.

"Should I honk?" I ask.

Eleanor snaps a few photos. "They're really taking their time, aren't they?"

As we wait for the sheep to cross, we discuss the songs on the playlist Eleanor made. She's super depressed at the moment, which means she makes really good ones.

"This is so sad that it's absolutely wonderful," I tell her. We've fogged up the windows, plastered with raindrops, listening to George Michael and Jewel and other hits from our childhood. "I would love to have this playing at my funeral. If something happens to me on this trip while driving, can you make that happen?" I just hope we make it to the Glen of Imaal region in County Wicklow so that I can see Ronan's homeland. I love that my dog originates from here. Hundreds of years ago, the French brought their long-bodied hounds to Ireland, who rendezvoused with the scruffy local terriers. It makes me wonder how much of Ireland has changed since then. The country looks untouched by time.

As much as I don't like driving in Ireland, it really is the best way to see the countryside. When we disobey our GPS and take the back roads, the good scenery appears: deserted ivy-covered castles and friendly local dogs who roam dirt roads and run right up to our car doors. We greet them with welcome squeals, even though we have no idea where we are in Ireland or in life for that matter.

"Recalculating!" says you-know-who at every wrong turn.

Our GPS is ruthless, without a sense of humor, not a kind bone in her electronic body. One little missed turn, and as punishment, she says the R-word, then takes us down a one-lane road that's so narrow with such limited visibility that a sign advises we honk to alert cars coming at us.

"Seriously?" I ask, after accidentally wedging our car between two stone walls. "She couldn't just turn us around on the main road?"

A couple of muddy locals navigate us out, all smiles. Eleanor and I laugh, then speed off to destroy another village.

"Try looking out both your side mirrors," she says, with the apathetic enthusiasm of a driving instructor. "Just try to keep the car between the white lines behind you."

I try really hard to think of our lives as a coloring book, where one accidental slip outside the lines will result in death, but Eleanor's tip doesn't work for me. I nearly sideswipe a car in a small village and miss another roundabout turn. Our GPS drops us somewhere we haven't expected to land, then when we try to correct course, she intervenes again. "Recalculating."

It's dark by the time we land in Galway for the night. We drop our bags off at our Airbnb, then head to a dimly lit pub in the center of town, with multicolored lights dangling from the ceiling. Tourists and locals stand shoulder to shoulder, pints in hand. I toss my winter coat onto an empty booth. A man tapping his toe to a peppy fiddle swoops in to stop me. He's wearing a bright orange sweater and has blue eyes, rosy cheeks, and full lips. I wish he were small enough to fit in my suitcase.

"My friend and I were already eyeing that booth—you'll have to share with us," he says with a wink.

We buy each other so many rounds that I'm not sure whether I've had too much vodka or if the live Irish music is actually so loud that it rattles the old photos on the wooden walls.

"I'm a New Yorker!" I yell.

He grabs my hand for a dance. "I'm a bartender!"

Perfect. We wedge ourselves into the crowd to imbibe under the glow of Christmas lights, and I toss my arms around his broad shoulders. At the end of the night, we stumble home together. It isn't the first time I've had sex since my marriage ended, but it is the first time I've had sex in Ireland, something I wish there was a stamp for in my passport. He leaves before daylight with my number in his pocket, and over breakfast, Eleanor and I piece the evening back together while trying to hold down our orange juice and eggs, wishing that one of us had been smart enough to bring ibuprofen.

"Do you think he'll text you?" Eleanor asks.

"I doubt it. What is there to say? Thanks for the sex? Have a good life?"

My friend Aine, who was born here, always says that Ireland isn't real life. It's a place where you have lots to drink and marvel at the scenery—the men, above all—and then you go back rejuvenated to face reality.

"What pub did you say he worked at again?" Eleanor asks.

One Google search later, we cruise past his bar on our way out of town like the expert stalkers we've always been.

"Recalculating," our old friend says.

Eleanor dozes off in the passenger seat as I drive past castles hundreds of years old and try to photograph them while driving with one hand. There are plenty of rolling green fields, stitched together by stone walls that I come within inches from slamming us into. An angry driver's horn awakens Eleanor from her nap.

"What?" I say to her, staring straight ahead, pretending I have the situation under control.

When I've had enough of the GPS, I turn it off, surrendering to kismet and a cliffside one-lane road. We travel dangerously close to the edge along the choppy Atlantic, where jagged rocks jut out from the sea. I pull off at a deserted lookout point. We get out of the car and breathe in salty air at the edge of a cliff. Miles and miles of ocean separate me from life back in New York. We've stumbled onto Slea Head, the westernmost point of Ireland, even more majestic and moody than the Cliffs of Moher, and not a soul in sight. Angry waves crash against the cliffs. A dark raincloud hovers offshore. You'd never find this gem in a travel book.

It occurs to me that driving in Ireland is not unlike my life in New York. I've been trying to move ahead but really I'm just traveling in circles, from an apartment with cockroaches to an apartment with mice, from one soul-sucking job to another, from a bad date to "what's a date?" I'm not getting anywhere, no matter how hard I try. I had always thought I'd stay in New York forever, but in order to get back on the straight and narrow, I think I need to make a change, a really big one.

I tuck my numb fingers in my coat pockets. Eleanor snaps a few photos. "Ready to go?"

Keys in hand, I climb into the driver's seat. Another dark pub and a hot Irishman are calling my name. I don't know where we're going to end up, but I feel like we'll find our way.

Moving to My Dog's Hometown

Careful not to flash the camera, I adjust the deep V-neck on my dress, a silky red number that I saw in a storefront window but never had a reason to wear until now. It feels like a special occasion coming back to Magic Jewelry in Chinatown to have our aura photos taken. Maybe I should get a crystal today too.

"I can't believe you're leaving New York!" Annie says, leaning an elbow on the glass countertop.

"I can," Sarah replies. "You were miserable at work. It's time for something different!"

The store is bustling with customers, even though we've shown up at opening time. I love coming here. I feel like I'm with my people.

"Okay, so tell us the story again," Bridget says, brushing her bangs to the side. Her aura photo came back red again. "Did they shit their pants when you told them you were leaving?"

"They were pretty surprised. I gave them two weeks' notice."

"I can't believe you didn't tell us first," Bridget says.

"I didn't know I was going to quit until that day. Annie gave me a little push." And thank God she did.

We had gone out for a lunchtime walk after a terrible morning at work. I had been incorporating a client's feedback into something I wrote, but I forgot to check off each request as I addressed it and couldn't remember at the end of the project what I had fixed and what I hadn't. Such a simple task, but it was the closest I had ever come to being fired. Maybe my subconscious was trying to do me a favor. I wanted to quit more than anything but couldn't find the courage.

It was a hot summer afternoon, the worst time of year to be trapped in the city. Annie and I crossed Sixth Avenue. One World Trade Center came into view, which made me think of Jack. When we first started dating, we used to pass the construction site on our way to his old apartment. I took Ronan to dog parks downtown and watched the building go up, floor by floor. I hoped our marriage would be in a better place when it was finally built.

On the day it finally opened, we had a drink at the bar up top. My ears popped on the zippy elevator ride, over a hundred flights. We could see for miles through the glass walls, all the way to Brooklyn. It should have felt celebratory, but it felt like there was a finality to the day.

I knew that as long as I lived in New York, as long as I could see the building's spire, I'd be reminded of my failed marriage. I had always been able to move to another neighborhood or another borough after a breakup and reinvent myself, but this time felt different. Seeing the World Trade Center again with Annie on our walk, I thought, *How great would it be to never have to see it again? How great would it be to never have to obsess over client feedback in a Google Doc again?*

If there's anything my mother's death and my MS diagnosis taught me, it's that life is too short to waste time doing what you hate. But was it crazy to quit my job without another terrible job to catch me?

The rest of the afternoon, as my coworkers laughed in the kitchen and walked back and forth to meetings, I practiced in my head what I might say to my boss. I knew that if I could just get the first sentence out of my mouth, there was no taking it back. I opened the glass door to the conference room, sat down in the chair across from my boss, and placed my notebook on the table.

"I've decided to quit," I said. Ten minutes later, I walked out of the conference room on a new path.

"That's so badass," Bridget says, waving her Polaroid. "But are you sure about New England and moving in with Susan and Jake?"

Susan was excited when I told her that I had quit my job and wanted to leave New York. I had thought I'd never see Susan and Jake again after Jack and I sped off with Ronan, but to my surprise, we stayed in touch. It feels easier to talk to her about my divorce than to many of my friends who are married with children.

My move turned out to be perfect timing for both of us. She and Jake were making some changes too. They had recently retired and were remodeling their house to make the bottom floor its own apartment.

"Come here!" she said. "Stay until you figure out what you want to do. You can be our first tenant!"

I remembered how cute I thought Hanover was when we picked up Ronan; I just never thought I'd want to live there. But the more I thought about it, the more I realized it made sense. I could pay less in rent and have a fenced-in yard for Ronan, plus a washer and dryer. I didn't have a full-time job lined up, but I had already been doing some freelance writing on the side, which could cover me for a while. It was a wild decision but easier to trust it because of Ronan. It was his hometown after all. And it would give me what I really wanted: a life unlike the one I had. I didn't want to live in another big city. I didn't want to work in another tall office building, disconnected from the world around me.

Susan called me practically every day after I said I was coming.

"Do you have dishes?" she asked one day. I was knee-deep in packing, boxes arranged high around me like Jenga pieces. One wrong move, and they'd all fall over.

"I have dishes, but not that many," I said, grabbing the tape dispenser out of Ronan's mouth. "You know I don't cook. It disturbs the mice in my oven."

"What about a television?"

Was she going to be this hands-on when I moved into her house? Maybe. Susan's bossiness was one of the things that put me off when we first met four years ago when Jack and I picked up Ronan. She told me that the dog collars and leashes I brought were wrong. Apparently, a harness was a big no-no. She told me that my sandals were not to be used as a chew toy for Ronan.

"Can you believe how bossy she was?" I asked Jack in the car as we sped back to New York City, Ronan sleeping in the back seat.

He laughed. "Don't worry," he replied, patting my knee. "You'll never have to see her again."

Funny how life turns out. I never *had* to see Susan again, but I wanted to. And I thought I'd be married forever, but the reality is, I'll probably never see my ex-husband again after I move.

Sarah slides her Polaroid onto the glass counter. Hers is still a hodgepodge of colors, with only a few slight differences. The more obvious change is that she's changed her hairstyle again, this time to a bright blonde pixie cut.

"What did your dad say about your move?" she asks.

He weighed the odds, like usual. He brought up all the reasons I should stay in New York. Why would I want to leave my friends and a stable job with health insurance? His doubts are the same ones I have. Am I being irresponsible, or am I being bold? Why do I still feel like I need my father's approval, even though I'm a grown woman? I'll just have to go my own way and hope it works out.

"He thinks I'm crazy," I say. "And no matter how many times I tell him I'm moving to New Hampshire, he keeps asking me why I'm moving to Massachusetts."

Annie laughs. "I'm going to miss the hell out of you. So will the mice in your apartment."

What's strange is that since I made my decision to leave New York, the mice haven't turned up. Maybe it's just warmer out, and they've found somewhere nicer outside to be. Or maybe they were chasing me out for a reason?

"Whoa, look at your aura photo!" Annie says.

Whoa is right. We lean in for a closer look. It looks nothing like my old one. Orange and yellow hues hover above my head like a halo. I wave down a woman behind the counter to find out what it means. The woman glances at my photo, then tells me I'm tapping into my third chakra, my personal power. This feels so right to me. I might not know exactly what I want, but I know what I don't want, and that's spending the rest of my life working as a ghostwriter, trying to sound like someone else, even if it's a steady paycheck.

The black cloud that was in my last photo has also disappeared. It feels like I'm thinking clearly now, even though it probably looks like I've lost my mind to everyone around me, having cut ties to everything I know. I had always wondered where I might go after New York. Abroad? The West Coast? Never did I think I'd want to move to a small town in New England. Maybe I would have done it sooner if I hadn't been waiting for someone to give me permission to upend my life, but no one could give me that, not even Annie. I had to do it myself.

 I can't think of a more perfect way to say goodbye to New York than one last aura photo. Annie lines all of our Polaroids together on the glass countertop, then takes a picture of them with her phone. I swipe my Polaroid off the counter to give it another look. I love my new photo. It looks as if I've lit myself on fire.

FOLIAGE SEASON

No Questions. Just Yell.

I'm staring at the ceiling of my new apartment, trying to figure out why Susan and Jake are yelling out the same word at exactly the same time. And then it hits me. They're watching *Jeopardy!* on TV.

I wander upstairs and find them in the living room, relaxing in their chairs facing the television, martinis in hand. Cheese and crackers are spread out on the breakfast bar. I can't see the television because it's blocked by one of Jake's beloved bamboo trees strung up in multicolored lights. I can't hear the television either, not with how much yelling is happening in the living room, the profanity that spills out of Susan and Jake's mouths when they miss easy questions about US states, herbs, baseball teams, and American senators. Who knew *Jeopardy!* was so much fun? Is this what my marriage would have looked like if Jack and I had made it thirty years like Susan and Jake did?

All five dogs rush to the landing to greet me, whereas Susan and Jake barely look my way. They're so into the game that they never check their phones and can barely remember how much time is left on the chicken in the oven. *Jeopardy!* seems far more interactive than *Antiques Roadshow*, the Monday-night fare Jack and I watched in New York, where we tried to guess if the items on the screen were really valuable or "worth fuck all," as Jack used to say. We also liked *Shark Tank*, where regular people pitched their business ideas. Funny to think that the game shows Jack and I liked were based on trying to figure out how much something was worth. I was doing the same thing in our marriage.

Susan slaps her thigh. "I can't believe we didn't get that answer right. You went to Yale!"

Jake laughs. "You went to law school!"

Yale? Law school? I have a degree in journalism. What good is that going to do me here?

"Aren't you supposed to provide the answer in the form of a question?" I ask.

Susan shushes me, then circles back around at the next commercial break. She mutes the television.

"Listen, we have our own routine here. If you want to play, you have to follow our rules. Whoever yells it first wins. No questions. Just yell."

Yelling out answers feels therapeutic, even if they're embarrassingly wrong. I'm one of those people with severe gaps in my memory for American history, geography, and other topics I should remember from grade school. Still, a half hour with Alex Trebek is far better than what I had been doing earlier in the day: staring out the window wondering if this was a really stupid decision, moving to Hanover with no plan. So far, I haven't done much more than take Ronan on long walks to check out the neighborhood or grab a coffee in town. I love it when Susan invites me upstairs. Her house is the kind of snug abode you'd want to wake up in when it's snowing outside. It's super cozy, with a white stucco fireplace, Oriental rugs, and framed photos of the kids adorning the walls.

I plop down on the couch. Susan's dog Picabo leaps on top of me, then uses her paw to tap my thigh and steal my attention. She pops up into a sit, resting on her hind legs so I'll rub her belly.

"You're an attractive nuisance," Susan says.

"I don't know how you get anything done. I'd just sit here and pet them all day."

"We don't need to get anything done. We're retired now."

I rub Picabo between her ears; her eyes float back in her head. I stop, but then she uses her paw to tap my arm again. A little pink tongue flops out of her mouth. "Who's that pretty girl!"

"Be careful with that dog voice," Susan warns. No sooner does she say this than Ronan's pathetic whine creeps up through the floorboards. "I told you. He knows you're cheating."

I don't even bother asking if Ronan can come upstairs. Last time we tried that, he ran around the living room and tried to hump his sister.

A clue flashes across the screen.

Don't overcook the pasta—I like it "to the tooth."

"Al dente!" I yell.

Susan shoots me a look that says *bitch*.

"I guess I know my carbs."

I come back for *Jeopardy!* the next night and the night after that. It provides the camaraderie and routine that I sorely need. Jake is good at baseball. Susan really knows her airport codes. I could be a Beatle, given how well I know their lyrics. We share the details of our day over commercial breaks. It amazes me how much you can fill your day with doing, well, nothing.

Phone calls and texts roll in from friends in New York to check in on my wild decision to move north. Annie and Bridget say that work has gotten even worse, which is hard to believe.

"There's not enough smoky quartz crystals to make this place any more tolerable," Annie says.

My father calls from Ohio. "So, what's it like up there in Massachusetts?" he asks.

"I live in New Hampshire."

"New Hampshire. Well, what are you doing for fun?"

I tell him that I'm winning at *Jeopardy!* in food and beverage categories. Turns out that the cocktail knowledge I gained from eleven years of drinking in New York City helps in the *Drinks All Around!* category, devoted entirely to alcohol. Susan, Jake, and I do so well that we miss only one question, about the ingredients in a Dry Rob Roy. Even Jake, the martini expert, is stumped. "Put that one on the list for us to try," he says.

Usually, I wander upstairs around 6:30 p.m. before the show begins, hoping to piggyback off of whatever Susan has made for dinner. Other times I send a text if I don't hear activity upstairs, which is rare. My first morning here I realized I would probably have to move if sleeping late ever became important to me. The upstairs deck is right above my bedroom and happens to be the same tarmac where all of Susan and Jake's dogs charge outside every morning to do their business. I moved from New York hoping for a little peace and quiet, but I've yet to find it. Most of the time I'm not sure if Susan is yelling at Jake or the dogs when I hear, "Be quiet! Enough! Get off me!"

One evening, I arrive just in time for Alex Trebek to reveal the category for *Final Jeopardy!*: *The Novel*.

No Imperial Russia? No mythology? I straighten up on the couch. Even the dogs can sense the anticipation.

Jake leans toward Susan. "You got this. No one I know reads as much as you."

That's true. Susan has been known to piss off the Hanover librarians for taking out ten books at a time. The clue pops up.

I collected the instruments of life around me, that I might infuse a spark of being into the lifeless thing that lay at my feet.

"FRANKENSTEIN!" I yell. The dogs go wild, tails thumping against the floor. Ronan starts barking from downstairs. "I WON! YEAH!" I even do a little dance around the coffee table. I can't believe how good winning feels.

"You didn't give me a chance!" Susan yells. "Next time, we'll write down our answers ahead of time."

"You said that whoever yells out the answer first wins!"

"How'd you know that answer anyway?" she asks.

"I just read a *New Yorker* story about Mary Shelley. It's the book's two hundredth anniversary." That's one upside of being unemployed. I've had plenty of time to read.

"Can I have the magazine when you're done with it? Maybe we can share a subscription."

Something tells me that Susan wouldn't be okay with grease-covered pages, which is what usually happens when I sit down to read it with some kind of snack in my hands.

"Did you know Mary Shelley was only eighteen when she started writing *Frankenstein*?"

This is who I am now. A monster competitor who stores away valuable trivia knowledge in the hopes that one day it will come in handy for my new favorite game show.

Later that night when I get in bed, the sound of muffled laughter upstairs in the kitchen seeps through the heating vents. I fall asleep convinced that *Jeopardy!* would have saved my marriage. Maybe Jack and I were just one click of the remote away from staying together.

You Got a Deal

A car salesman slides a piece of paper across the desk with monthly payment figures for a Jeep Cherokee. Susan crosses out the numbers, then leans back in her chair. Before Susan retired, she was a divorce lawyer who never lost a case in her entire career. These men won't even know what hit them.

"Too high," she says. "*This* is what we'll pay."

I've come to the Jeep dealership today to buy a car, the first order of business that a New Yorker needs upon leaving the kingdom. I'm so excited about finally breaking free from crowded subway rides and commuting through sloppy snow and rain puddles and carrying my laundry up four flights of stairs that I can barely control myself. Broken grocery bags be gone forever! I've never had a new car in my life, and I feel like there isn't a better time to treat myself to one.

I had no idea where to start. Lease? Buy? I didn't know the first thing about a new car purchase, only that I wanted a Jeep Wrangler, and no one was going to talk me out of it—not even Susan.

"Why don't you buy Joe's old Toyota?" Susan said when I arrived in Hanover.

That wasn't how I saw myself, driving around in a beat-up car covered in rust and old bumper stickers. I wanted something new, something I wouldn't have to sage bad spirits out of. I felt a Jeep Wrangler suited me, perfect for a girl from the Empire State, new to town and ready to navigate rugged terrain. I certainly wasn't sporty—I didn't even know how to ski. But at least if I had the car, I'd look like I did all the winter sports that actually terrified me.

I imagined how cute Ronan would look in the passenger seat of my new Wrangler with the top down and his big head hanging out the window. Plus, there would be plenty of room in the back seat for making out with lumberjacks.

I had no idea how much it cost to buy a Jeep Wrangler, but I figured I could afford a lease payment if all the Dartmouth College kids were driving them around town. When the salesman said the model that I wanted retailed for close to $40,000, I realized that Dartmouth students were not the ones actually buying the cars and that I would not be getting a Jeep Wrangler. But maybe I could afford a used Jeep Cherokee the color of a blueberry?

"So, are you in or out?" the salesman asks. "We've already taken $50 off your monthly payment. We can't go any lower."

Susan swipes the piece of paper off the desk. "We'll think about it."

A bell on the door dings as we leave. A gust of wind blows an empty seltzer can across the parking lot. We tighten our jackets. Black rain clouds hover above, ready to unleash.

"Now what?" I ask. My dream Wrangler catches my eye, perched high on a ramp above the other Jeeps. I wish I could take it for a test drive and keep it forever. "I have no car."

"Can we do that full moon ceremony thing you always talk about even when the moon isn't full? Maybe we can manifest you a car tonight."

"Or find a bank to rob so I can get my Jeep Wrangler?"

"Listen, Betsy. We had to walk away. It's the only way to instill fear."

"Then why am I the one who's scared?"

Back home, I continue unpacking. I find the box with the childhood scrapbooks my mother made for me and slide it into the closet. When I try to close the door, it jams. Unpacking seems so much more time-consuming than packing. I look around at all the boxes, wonder what's inside them, and wish I had labeled them better. I crawl into bed and turn off the light. I pull Ronan up close to me. His breath smells. My phone flashes and lights up the dark room. It's Susan.

Don't worry. We'll get you a car.

I awake early the next morning to the usual thunderous running of the dogs above my bedroom. I take a quick shower and head upstairs.

I'm exhausted, but Susan is smiling and full of energy. At least one of us slept well. She slides the newspaper across the counter and points to an ad.

"There's a deal on at Toyota," she says, pouring CBD oil into her thermos of coffee to calm her anxiety before another battle. "Let's see what the sexist jerks there can do for us."

The lot at Toyota is full of cars, lined up side by side like colorful gumdrops. They should be paying *me* to take them off their hands and put some miles on them. Inside the dealership, no one at their cubicles looks up from their computers when we walk through the door.

"Can someone actually help us? We want to buy a car!" Susan yells to the room.

A young blond man with a nearly dead goldfish on his desk waves us over. Susan sets her purse on the floor. "At Jeep, they came right out. What the hell are you guys doing here anyway?"

The young man shuffles a few papers, then introduces himself as Sully.

"Like the pilot who landed the airplane in the Hudson?" I ask.

"That's right," he replies. "Except I sell cars. What are you in the market for?"

A lot of things. A boyfriend, a job, sex . . . "I think I might want to sit up high. I suffer from short-leg syndrome, like my dog."

What kind of car would Ronan like? I guess having four doors would be nice so he could get in and out easily, but all he'll really care about is being able to hang his head out the window. "If it's cheaper to have two doors instead of four, let's do that."

"You sound like you might be a RAV4 girl!"

I am absolutely not a RAV4 girl. The dashboard inside the SUV feels overwhelming, like having to explain why you got divorced. Too complicated. I size up all the knobs and numbers, trying to figure out how I feel about it. The inside smells fresh, full of possibilities and accidents to be had. I don't know what I am doing, other than hoping I won't ruin anything. It's been a long time since I've been in a new car. I never had a touch screen, sunroof, leather seats, or keyless entry. Susan is cruising next to me in the passenger seat, though Sully doesn't seem to mind being relegated to the back. I pull out onto the road. Even the turn signal sounds new, its click soft and delicate, as if operating inside a library.

"Should we get breakfast?" Sully asks. "McDonald's?"

"You buying?" I ask.

"I will if you take this car. How about we take a spin on the highway?"

"I'd rather not. Can't we just take the back roads?"

After eleven years of not driving a car in New York City, I want to ease back into it. This whole thing is eerily reminiscent of when I was sixteen and learning how to drive. I assumed my mother would take me to the empty parking lot of our local grocery store and let me cruise around, but she had me get into the driver's seat and pull out onto our busy street, even though I had no idea what I was doing. I pressed my right foot down on the gas and hovered my left on the brake.

"STOP!" she yelled.

I swerved off the road so that she could explain lesson number one of driving: Use your right foot for both the gas and the brake. This made no sense. Why make one foot do all the work?

After that, she enrolled me in driver's ed with a cute guy named Kerry. He must have been at least a decade older than me, but I still thought I had a chance with him. I never had a boy pick me up in a car before, so when his car appeared in my driveway, it felt like a date, even if the car had a sign on the roof that said: STUDENT DRIVER.

"I think I'm in love with him," I confessed to my mother.

She laughed. "What you love is what he's doing for you. He's teaching you how to be free."

She was right about that. I wanted to drive myself to the movies and to high school football games. I was sick of being the passenger, of having to ask someone to drive me when I wanted to go somewhere. I needed a car then as much as I need one now.

As I try to park Sully's car, I think about all the parallel parking skills Kerry taught me. I know I have plenty of room, but the new touch screen won't stop beeping.

"Can we turn that thing off?"

"I don't think so," Sully says, staring at the monitor. He doesn't know how to use it either.

"Cross this one off the list then." I glance behind me a couple of times, then slide the car right into a narrow spot.

"Wow, that's impressive," Sully says, unbuckling his seat belt. "You know, I sure do like older women. Real take-charge."

I toss the keys into his lap. "What makes you think I'm older?"

"The birthdate on your driver's license that you gave me."

After driving a couple more cars, Susan and I narrow my choices down to a hybrid SUV. I assume Sully will take my name and social security number and let me float out with a new car like on *The Price Is Right*, but I'm handed a stack of paperwork that must have killed a thousand trees.

"Great choice," Sully says, as I get out a pen. "Your mom likes it too."

My mom? "Are you talking about Susan? She's not my mom."

"Oh, I just assumed she was. You guys seem to have that whole mother-daughter thing going on."

"Speaking of Susan, where is she?"

She's hovering over another salesman's cubicle, trying to get my monthly payment down like she did at the Jeep dealership. Now that I think about it, I have to admit that Susan feels a lot like my mother, who walked into a parent-teacher conference and talked my high school teacher out of giving me a detention for letting another girl copy my homework.

"So, what now?"

Sully says there's a secret back room, tucked away from the hubbub, where the Wizard of Toyota decides whether I am a suitable candidate for a loan, whether I can click my heels three times and go home with my new car. I worry that I won't be approved, but Sully assures me that anything with a pulse can get approved, even the goldfish on his desk.

"Trust me," Sully laughs. "A dead body could get a loan these days! The only time you have to worry is when I walk out of the room sweaty and red-faced."

An hour later, Sully emerges from the back room, red-faced and sweaty, and I wonder if I'm in trouble. Is my credit bad? I should've checked my credit score before coming here. I dumped most of my savings into that mouse-infested apartment from hell and racked up my credit cards from egg-freezing. I traveled to Ireland for sex and moved all my things three-hundred miles north. The more I think about it, buying a new car sounds like a really bad idea. Who knows how long I'll be living in Hanover?

I pull Susan aside. "Let's get out of here."

"What? Why? Are you sure? We can't just leave. I got my own car here. They'll never talk to me again!"

I grab my tote bag off the floor. Sully panics. "I'm sorry for the wait!" he yells. This is a salesman's worst nightmare, watching you walk out the door. "I'll call you when I hear from the bank!"

On the drive home, nostalgia creeps in, and I find myself pining for New York. I didn't need to go through all of this to live there. The subway was only $100 a month, and included everything, even the occasional glimpse of a man's penis.

Susan turns onto our street. "What do you think happened? In that back room?"

"Don't know," I say, staring out the window. "I should have a better plan for my future. I still don't have my shit together."

"Listen, Betsy, getting our shit together is a lifelong process and does not happen overnight. It's a process we have to engage in for the rest of our lives."

"Maybe I should go back to New York."

"Why don't you just buy Joe's old car?"

Susan has raised this possibility before, but it's the first time I'm really listening to her. Joe's Toyota Corolla lets off more emissions than a coal-fired power plant and has bumper stickers that have been there so long that they have actually morphed into the paint, but I guess that car is better than a bicycle and my two legs. Maybe I could put my own bumper stickers on it or get vanity plates to make it feel like mine.

"What year is it?"

"2002."

Another time I journeyed into the unknown, the same year I graduated college and followed a boyfriend out west to Colorado. My mother had been dead for two years. I didn't even attend my graduation ceremony. Without her, I couldn't. I was worried about the future then too, but it all worked out fine. Maybe I should just buy the Corolla and see what happens.

Susan and Jake are firm on $2,000, but I know there are plenty of problems with the car that I could argue about to try and get a lower price. The cup holder is broken and so is the handle on the driver's-side door. There's a huge dent on the back left side and so many miles on the odometer that I'm sure I'm reading it wrong. Can it really be over 150,000, or do I need my eyes checked?

I know I should try and negotiate, but I've seen what Susan did to the car salesmen. Plus, they agree to throw in four clunky things in the trunk called snow tires. I'm not sure if I really need them, but when I question going without them, Susan laughs.

"You got a deal," I say.

Sully calls the next day to tell me I've been approved for a loan, but it's too late. I'm already taking my new used car out for a spin to King Arthur Bakery to celebrate with a breakfast sandwich. What surprises me more than everything that's wrong with my car is that I'm absolutely fine with driving it. Buying this old car reminds me of what my mother said about my driving instructor: he's teaching you how to be free.

This car is teaching me how to be free too. I'm not burdened by a car payment every month, which means I can spend more on lattes and beefing up my New England wardrobe of sweatpants and flannel. I'm free from guilt when Ronan bounds into the car covered in mud and drools all over the passenger seat. Who cares about scratch marks when the door handle doesn't even work right? There's no complicated touch screen complaining about my driving skills, no heated seats using up all my battery power. But above all, what I love most about the car is that it's truly mine. I didn't have to ask my father or a bank for help. Every time I glance out my side mirror and see nothing but the joy on Ronan's face, his pink tongue whipping in the wind, it feels like I finally did something right.

BOOM!

"Find me a man," I say, handing my phone to Susan. I've just opened up Bumble, a dating app.

"Now?" Susan asks, looking around the small hospital room where I'm having one of my monthly medication infusions. Machines beep and whir around us.

I've been treating my multiple sclerosis this way for several years now. There's usually another patient in the room with me if I'm alone, but Susan's big personality takes up the empty space when she accompanies me, and the nurses know by now to never subject another patient to Susan. That said, I like bringing her along. I don't have to explain any of the medical stuff to her. She's a breast cancer survivor, and she knows from her own chemo treatments how painful it is to have a nurse poke and prod your veins to find a winner. I try to tell my veins to cooperate, but I think that only makes them more stressed out.

"We need your *best* person on her," Susan instructed a nurse the first time I brought her. "Tiny veins. I was the same way. You might want to use the needles you use on children."

I used to bring Jack with me to my infusion appointments, but after we divorced, I went alone. Other couples across the room held hands and spoke in loving whispers, the way he and I had done. The only thing worse than being single is being sick with no one to take care of you.

It's been interesting coming to these appointments with Susan. A lot of the time, they feel like therapy sessions for both of us.

"Do you think I should get a part-time job now that I'm retired?" Susan asks.

Even though I'm in a different phase of my life, there are plenty of similarities between our circumstances. Neither of us knows what to do next. I had always thought that life got easier, the path more certain with time. It's a relief to learn that I'm not the only one who's lost.

"How would you ever find time to read all your library books and bake bread if you had a part-time job? Here's a harder question for you. Do you think I'll ever find a boyfriend?"

The biggest problem I've had with trying to date in a small town is the available dating pool. Surely, there must be older professor types at Dartmouth. Even better if they like dogs and carbs. But where are they?

Anytime I'm out and about, I tell people that I'm single and looking. One time, three older women approached me at a coffee shop and asked if I would take their picture. I obliged, but not before asking if they knew any single men.

"Any single *straight* men?" one of the women clarified.

I nodded, and she laughed.

"Oh, honey. This isn't a good town for single women your age."

Then where is? I remember before I left New York, I did a Google search to try and find the towns with the largest concentrations of single men. It turned out there were a lot in the Pacific Northwest, but it rains a lot there, so why not just go to Ireland then?

In truth, I think dating is hard everywhere. You've got to be in the right place at the right time. New York wasn't much better. Even though the dating pool was bigger, it still felt impossible to meet people. I'm starting to really crave companionship, and I wonder if swiping guys on a dating app will be easier if I do it with Susan.

"You might have some luck with online dating," she says. "My kids met all their polyamorous partners online."

That doesn't sound good. All I need is one boyfriend, not multiple. I open the dating app on my phone. Susan's chair squeaks as she leans forward to take a peek. "This is going to be fun! Let me grab my glasses."

I'm not having all that much fun right now. My arm feels sore from my IV line. I place it on a soft pillow, careful to not bump it. Before coming to the hospital for infusions, I injected myself with shots every few days. It's far better to come in once a month and then be done with it, except the problem now is that I won't be able to grab the phone out of Susan's hands if she does something she's not supposed to do.

"Dating is *not* fun," I say. "Just swipe to the left if he's bad and to the right if he's good. You don't have to show the men to me. I trust your judgment."

Susan has already tried to set me up with a man who owns a burger joint up here. Someone who likes to cook—absolutely my type. I wasn't with her, but she told me that she chatted him up at the restaurant, desperate to make it happen. I imagined Susan holding up the line, with frustrated customers behind her, while she waved photos of me on her phone in front of him.

"I reminded him that we all sat together at Bella's bat mitzvah," Susan said. "He remembered who you were, but he didn't seem interested. He said he had a girlfriend."

I appreciated the sentiment, but trying to set me up with someone who was taken didn't get me far then, and I'm not getting far now, watching Susan try to figure out the dating app.

"Left is good?" she asks.

"No! Left is bad."

If we're going to do this, maybe I should ask a nurse to hook me up to a heart monitor. Someone's medical line starts beeping a few doors down. A nurse pops into the room to see if it's me. It's not. She glances at my medicine bag. "I'd say you have about a half hour left. Do you want your chair reclined?"

"No thanks." I just want to get out of here and back into the world, even if it's a world with no available men.

"Is your blanket still warm? Want another one?" Susan asks. She knows I'm always cold, like Jake.

"I'm fine . . ."

"She'll take another blanket."

"Guess I'll take another blanket." I can't get used to Susan's maternal instincts, always wondering where I am and where I am going. What did I have for dinner? (Frozen pizza.) Had I talked to Jack at all? (Yes, to wish him happy birthday.) Did I want to come upstairs for a cocktail? (Always.)

"Okay, just let me know if you change your mind about the chair," the nurse says, zipping off down the hall, her sneakers squeaking on the shiny floor.

Susan returns my phone. I swipe through several guys in a few seconds.

"How can you tell that fast that you don't like a man? I had to give Jake plenty of chances to win me over. He messed up a lot in the beginning." She laughs. "And now look at us. I can't get rid of him!"

It feels hard to imagine that I'll ever meet someone good again, but I might as well try now. Of course, if it gets serious, I'll have to tell him about my illness, the way I had to tell Jack. I was so nervous to tell him. It was always a surprise to people because I didn't look sick. When Jack and I dated, I tried to keep my illness a secret in the beginning. I would even inject myself with my medication in his bathroom and then put the empty syringes back in my purse. When I finally decided to tell him, we were at a popular Asian restaurant on a Saturday night. There was a normalcy about the evening that just seemed appropriate. We were out to dinner like every other young couple in the restaurant. I waited for the familiar gasp of surprise that I was so used to from other people, but he responded with calm curiosity. His acceptance made me more willing to share the story of my illness with other people, like Susan, who's still staring at the Bumble app trying to figure it out. It's a lot more fun watching Susan try to figure out the app than it is to actually try and use it to get a date.

"Be ruthless," I say. "You're the one who always tells me to not settle."

A new photo pops up. "I'm swiping on this guy for you. He says he likes pizza."

"Okay, but is he cute?"

"I think so. What's your type?"

I don't think I have one. I've dated so many different kinds of men. Baldies, academics, writers, techies, number freaks. "Clearly, I have a thing for men from the British Isles..."

"Should I swipe right on pizza boy?" Susan asks.

I sigh. "Sure, go ahead." A bright yellow background pops up. Our photos flash together side by side as if we've belonged together our whole lives.

"What does the 'BOOM!' mean on the screen?"

"It means he liked my photo too."

"BOOM!" Susan yells, laughing uncontrollably.

My nurse rushes into our room, out of breath when she arrives. The nurse glances at me, then my medicine pump. "Are you okay?"

"Not really. I'm trying out online dating, and it's terrible. Do you know any single men? Doctors? Patients? Or is that a HIPAA violation . . ."

The nurse checks the bag with my medication to see how much is left. "You need to stop whatever it is you're doing in here. You're upsetting the other patients."

"I'm sorry."

The nurse closes the door. Susan and I erupt in laughter.

"Come on, this isn't so bad, is it?" Susan asks.

I guess not. It cracks me up that Susan's really taking her time, reading each profile in detail, as if it is a nutrition label with lots of unpronounceable substances. Of the ten available men who seem normal, don't have eyebrow piercings, and live in Hanover, I haven't liked any of them. Susan raises my mile limit from twenty miles to sixty miles and then again, to however many miles I think my 2002 Corolla will last without breaking down.

"Okay, come on, let's get you more BOOMs," Susan says. "This guy says he's an entrepreneur. That's good, right?"

"An entrepreneur? What's his business?"

"I don't know, but his profile says he attended the School of Hard Knocks."

"That means he's unemployed. Swipe left."

Another profile pops up. "Oooooooo . . . this guy is cute. He lives in Burlington. That's far. But his profile says he likes wine and cheese. That sure sounds like you."

My heart warms. Susan knows me, like *really* knows me. She knows I love anything that was made from a potato. She knows that I like spinach lasagna with crispy edges. She'd never dream of using chicken stock in a recipe for me because I've been a vegetarian since I was seven.

She swipes on wine-and-cheese boy. "You got another BOOM!"

My IV pump beeps. I'm done. It's time to go home. Susan's up and out of her chair, peeking her head out of the doorway to find a nurse to release me. "Let's get you out of here."

Susan is the perfect person to bring to the hospital with me. She knows that even though these hospital appointments seem routine, there's always a chance I'll get sick again and relapse, the same way she worries about her breast cancer returning. Who knows if I'll ever partner with another man in my life, but at least I have Susan. She's my real match.

Can I Bring My Dog to Work?

My hands are so sweaty that they're leaving wet marks on my navy dress. I shift in my uncomfortable wooden chair. I've always hated job interviews.

"Can you describe your writing process?" a woman asks, adjusting the cuffs on her blazer.

I guess my writing samples aren't enough for the Dartmouth interviewers across the conference room table from me. They want a behind-the-scenes look at how I put words on the page, but I've always found that trying to explain to a nonwriter how the magic happens is a little like asking a coroner about his creative process.

This is the first full-time job interview I've had since moving to Hanover. While the job-search process has been more dreadful than I remembered, I'm glad I left New York when I did. My old company has been laying people off. Surely, I would have been let go from that soulless job, probably one of the first. The only redeeming thing about working there was that they let me bring Ronan to the office. He used to circle the room, traveling from desk to desk, begging for a head rub. He'd follow me into conference rooms and fall asleep at my feet. Sometimes, he'd jump up into a chair as if it were his job to run the meeting.

When I saw a writing position at Dartmouth's engineering school, I applied right away—my one and only chance to catch college students doing the walk of shame every morning on my way to work and to hopefully become one of them.

Earlier this morning, I zipped myself into a dress for the first time since leaving New York. It was tighter than usual. No surprise, given how much I've been eating upstairs at Susan's. I blow-dried my hair and spritzed my neck with perfume, but the smell didn't sit well with Susan, who rolled down her window the moment I sat down in her passenger seat.

"Why are you still wearing pajama pants and house slippers?" I asked. "Did you just roll out of bed?"

"They're not house slippers. They're UGGs."

"But you're not even wearing socks." Was nine in the morning considered early if you were retired?

"Are you nervous?" she asked, rolling her window back up. "Did you have coffee?"

Of course I did. I've never tried cocaine or Red Bull, but I wondered if maybe I'd have to give one or the other a try to stay alert while being grilled by fourteen Dartmouth employees for four hours. I barely thought I'd get this interview after my first phone call with the recruiter, who couldn't hear me answer her questions with all the barking. "Do you need a second to get that under control?" she asked. I wanted to tell her there weren't enough peanut butter dog treats in the world to get six dogs under control.

Dartmouth's campus is only a mile up the road from the house, but Susan offered to give me a lift. On the short drive, we passed brick buildings and Dartmouth students carrying yoga mats. Nerds and jocks moseyed around in backpacks, texting and walking, on their way to study algorithms and create more terrible dating apps.

My apprehension sank deeper and deeper into my stomach the slower Susan drove. By the time she stopped the car, I wondered if vomiting during the interview would immediately disqualify me.

"Do I have to?" I asked, the engine still running.

She nodded, then sipped coffee from her thermos. "We're retired now, and we need your rent money."

I opened the door and brushed dog hair off my tights. *Oh, Ronan,* I thought. *How am I going to pay for your dog food and stuffies that you destroy in two minutes? What if I don't get this job? I have to provide for you.*

I've been staying afloat by freelancing for the local newspaper because I have news reporting experience from my time as a journalist. Getting work from the local newspaper was incredibly easy. I didn't even have to wear pantyhose. I sent over a few newspaper clips, and a few hours later, I was officially hired. I even got a press pass in the mail, just like old times when I was a twenty-six-year-old journalist for the Associated Press, my first job in New York City.

I had always fantasized about being a small-town reporter, out in the world, discovering new people and places, but I could never figure out how people made any money doing that. Maybe they just went into debt like I did in New York. Then again, no journalist ever writes for the money. I loved seeing my name in print and the adrenaline rush of beating an impossible deadline, the thrill of finding a story in an unexpected place.

The question is, will my freelance writing be enough to survive on? I have alimony from Jack, but that will run out in a year. I've been looking everywhere for work. I even pinned my business cards to the bulletin board in the grocery store, but no one has emailed me yet.

"You got this! Text me when it's over!" Susan yelled when she dropped me off, her Prius fading into the distance.

A woman led me into an enormous room where blinding sunlight cascaded in through large windows. I wasn't sure if there was a correct place to sit. The conference table could easily seat two dozen people.

Another woman brought me a glass of water. "Thank you," I said, my voice echoing in the room.

I sailed through round one and round two relatively unscathed, acing easy questions about my career path and previous jobs.

"I have experience writing news articles, press releases, and website copy," I said. "But I've never worked in an academic environment and would welcome the opportunity to do so."

I was doing great until a half dozen members of Dartmouth's fundraising team walked in the room for round three, single file, grasping their binders. They are not the writers, editors, and engineering experts I'd already met with but the people responsible for keeping Dartmouth's coffers full. I can tell that they want to know they are dealing with someone who knows how to make money—and they are sorely mistaken if they think I am their gal.

"What brings you here?" one of them asks.

"My divorce," I say. "And my dog. Have you heard of the Glen of Imaal terrier? His name is Ronan, and now I'm living in my dog breeder's basement apartment. Actually, she's the one who dropped me off here today. Maybe you know her? She and her husband used to own a computer store in town. Her name is—"

"What I mean is . . . why are you interested in this job?"

Money. I can't say that. Health insurance and access to hot professors? Can't say that either.

"I take great satisfaction in turning complicated material into language that everyone can understand."

I get a few head nods. Whew. "May I have a refill on my water?" My cheeks feel hot.

My friend Aine, an organized Virgo who works in HR and is an expert at interviewing, correctly predicted that someone would ask what I read.

"Well, I love reading my *New Yorker* magazine every week," I say.

Or at least I used to when I lived in the city and cozied up to the bar for a quiet glass of wine on Sunday afternoon. Those days are long gone. Maybe I should find a bar to go to after this interview.

"Oh, I read it too," a woman at the end of the table says.

"I have always dreamed of having my byline in there," I say.

"Did you read the article recently about North Korea and nuclear war?"

"I must have missed that one." I usually start with the cartoons.

Another woman scans my resume, then places her glasses on the table. "How do you get your story ideas?"

"Usually from the newspaper or from conversations I have. Sometimes, wine." I wink.

No one laughs.

"Just kidding!"

A few women nod their heads. Someone else is trying really hard to stay awake.

My interview feels a little like an out-of-body experience, where I know I am dying but am still fully conscious.

"Do you have any questions for us?" a woman asks.

Oh, shit. I haven't thought of any. And that's when it hits me—I haven't prepared because I don't really want this job, not even if it's going to pay my health insurance and credit card debt. This is why I left New York, to do something different with my career, to do my own thing. That's what I've enjoyed most about writing for the newspaper. I've covered blood drives and apple crops and written profiles on local cartoonists, chefs, high school students, bee experts, and priests. The paper barely has an online presence, but I feel so alive when I see my stories on the front page that I just can't say no.

I suppose freelancing is less secure than a full-time job, but I'd rather take a chance than sit at a desk job I don't love. I like managing my own time and that every day is different. Is any job secure anyway? Annie, Sarah, and Bridget have all left our old dumpster fire of a company. They've moved on to better things. Maybe freelancing is mine.

Someone would be lucky to have this Dartmouth job, but I'd be kidding myself if I thought I was a good fit for them. Unfortunately, I need to ask a question because they're all staring at me.

"Can I bring my dog to work?" I ask. "Back in New York, I took my dog Ronan to the office."

The women at the table exchange glances. "We don't usually allow that."

"Oh, okay. Well, thank you for this wonderful opportunity. When do you hope to make a decision by?"

One by one, they stand. A woman picks up her binder. "We'll let you know," she says.

Don't Forget to Take Your CBD

Susan squirts a few drops of CBD into a cup of coffee, then slides it across the counter in my direction. "Give it a try. It'll help you unwind after your interview."

It looks like Susan's day has been far more relaxing than mine. Half-open magazines are strewn across the coffee table. The dogs are sprawled out on the carpet for their third nap of the day. If I were at work right now back in New York City, I'd be on my third cappuccino of the day. It feels strange to be doing nothing in the middle of a weekday afternoon, especially with the slight buzz I have from one glass of wine.

"I don't think I'll like CBD."

"How will you know unless you try it?"

Good point, I guess. "Fine, one sip."

The coffee tastes minty and a little sour, not something I'd want to start my day with. I prefer my coffee with a lot of cream.

A breeze jangles the wind chime outside on the deck. Susan's dog Rooney rolls over onto her back and sighs. I hear you, honey.

I've arrived back at the house in a terrible mood and a little later than anticipated because I stopped off at Pine, the bar at the Hanover Inn, after my terrible job interview. I slip my black high heels off my sore feet and onto the floor, hoping I never have to wear them again. Floyd sniffs them, then balances on his back legs, hoping for a head rub.

Susan has changed out of her UGGs and pajama pants and into leggings, a cozy sweater, and pink sneakers. She pulls a barstool up to the counter. For being in her early sixties, Susan barely has any wrinkles.

I wonder if CBD helps with that? If so, maybe I should start now.

"I can't believe you walked a mile home in those terrible heels," Susan says. "I would've come to get you. I told you to call me when it was over. Why didn't you?"

"I needed to walk it off."

Plus, my stroll past the campus cemetery made me feel a little bit better, knowing that one day none of my struggles would matter.

"Call me next time."

I can't decide if Susan is being nosy or helpful, like my mother was when we went to Kmart to buy under-the-bed Tupperware containers before she sent me off into the world for college. "I needed some time to de-stress." Can she smell the wine on my breath? "My feet hurt. What kind of job would allow me to wear sweatpants all day?"

"You went to Pine, didn't you?" Susan says, leaning toward me to pick a few of Ronan's white dog hairs off my black blazer. "For a drink?"

"You got me. I went to Pine."

Susan might be nosy, but I kind of like that she's interested in my life. I felt the same way with my own mother. I loved being mothered, to know that someone was always looking out for me or thinking about me when I wasn't around. That was the worst part about her death, feeling like no one cared about me anymore.

"Did you meet anyone? Were there any nice-looking men there?"

No, and I'm starting to worry about finding them. I haven't seen many men my age since I've been here. I had assumed there'd be a few single professors wandering around in their tweed blazers in search of a mate, but so far all I've seen around town are baby boomers wearing wedding rings. I guess if it gets really bad, I could always turn to an undergrad?

"No men. Just me, a glass of white wine, and a grilled cheese sandwich."

"Was the sandwich good? I could make a better one than them. Bet they charged you $15 for a slice of cheese in between two slices of bread. Tell me how your interview went."

"Do I have to? I really don't want to relive that."

"What was so bad about it?"

"I overshared about my divorce. I don't know how fundraising at an Ivy League college works. I couldn't think of any good questions. Anything else?"

Susan points to my coffee cup. "Drink up. CBD is good for you. Trust me, I know all about this stuff. I'm a cancer survivor, remember?"

Susan usually says "I'm a cancer survivor" when she wants me to do something. How can I argue with a cancer survivor? And how am I in my thirties and being told what to do? What to drink and when to call for a ride? Does Susan think she's my mother? Is this what all mothers do? I can't remember. After seventeen years without mine, I'm not used to someone wondering where I am, what I'm doing, what I'm wearing. I can't imagine how nosy she'd be if I actually had a boyfriend. I wish my mother were here to help. I miss her all the time, especially on my birthday and Christmas, but lately I've been feeling her absence more. Maybe it's because I feel so alone here.

"Did you guys talk about money during your interview?" Susan asks.

Money. Now, that's a great, practical question that only a Capricorn would bring up. And she's spot-on.

"We didn't talk about salary. That's probably another bad sign. We never got that far. Am I supposed to be feeling something with the CBD? I still feel pretty stressed."

"Keep drinking. I'll give you a bottle, and you can take it every morning with your coffee. I get my CBD at a discount through my medical marijuana dealer. Do you think your father would like some?"

"Can't you just give me whatever is in your liquor cabinet instead?"

"How'd you know where we keep our liquor?"

"I'm up here for *Jeopardy!* every night."

"I wonder who else they interviewed. Who the hell could be better than you?"

Now *that* I can agree with. "Who knows? Someone who went to Dartmouth maybe?"

"Well, don't count yourself out yet, Ohio girl. And don't forget to write thank-you emails. That's always important. And don't forget to open the washer door when you're finished with it. You closed it again."

Another push from her with the coffee cup. I'm going to need to drink CBD like water if she keeps nagging me like this. After living in New York City, where I had to lug my clothes to the laundromat, I thought I would relish having a washer and dryer at my own disposal. I hadn't expected them to come with specific instructions.

"You know, most people close the washer door when they're done," I say.

"If you haven't noticed already, Jake and I aren't most people. That's why there's a label on the front of the washer that says, *Keep Door Open*. And don't forget to clean the lint catcher in the dryer. Jake likes a good clean lint catcher."

God, Jake would die without his label maker. He's already used it to put my name on the mailbox, the Tupperware containers in the garage, Susan's spice containers in the kitchen. I just want this day to be over. Maybe I should just go back to Pine. If I sit on a barstool long enough, someone good would have to eventually walk in, unless I fall off it first?

"Lint catcher. Got it. Well, I think I'm going to go back downstairs now . . ."

"You should check your mailbox on your way down. You have mail. Jake checked for you."

I think I'm going to lose my mind. Who actually goes into other people's mailboxes? "Isn't that illegal? Checking my mail?"

"I don't think he was reading it. He just wanted to check it to see if it was there."

"I think that's the same thing. Maybe he can pay all my credit card bills for me then."

"You can ask him about it when he gets back. He'll be here soon. He said he wants to discuss the way you recycle. He says you aren't following the number system on the bottom."

At least when I lived in New York, all I needed to know was whether something was paper or plastic, but in Susan's house, recycling is far more complicated. Now I need to pay closer attention to the boxes marked one and two, though that's pretty easy. Those are the ones that usually contain my Cabot spreadable cheese and Ben & Jerry's ice cream.

Really, what's more worrisome than my recycling habits and Susan and Jake's parenting techniques is what's going to happen to me if I don't get more work. My savings are running out, and I'm paying $900 a month for health insurance, though my alimony is covering that for now.

"I think you should keep freelancing," Susan says. "Reach out to the woman at the business school you met on LinkedIn, and tell her you need more assignments. If you were only interested in the Dartmouth job for the paycheck, then it wasn't the right fit. I know it hasn't been easy, but do you really think you'd like that job anyway?"

I can't argue with her. It would be like making the same mistake twice. "They wouldn't even let me bring Ronan to the office!"

"Maybe you need your own business. Then, you can make the rules. Jake and I brought our dogs to work all the time at the computer store we owned. If only Rooney could sell iPhones and iPads too!"

"But what about health insurance? It's so expensive, but I need it for my multiple sclerosis medication."

"Would your dad help? Just until you get your bearings more?"

I want to do this on my own, without help, but he would if I asked him to. I hope I don't get to that point, but he'd be there if I asked. I'd probably get a lecture, though.

"This is just so much harder than I thought it would be."

"Well, you're in luck. I love playing the role of fixer. I do it for all my friends."

It would be amazing if Susan could somehow solve all my problems, but it's going to take a lot more than CBD. I'll have to cut down on my expenses. No more mail-order wine clubs. I'll dial down the haircuts and highlights and online shopping—whatever I can do to make this work. At least I don't have a car payment. Maybe I can sell my old New York dresses on eBay. I've already been dog-walking on the side for Susan's other Glen people in town. Maybe Jake can make me more business cards with his label maker.

"Don't worry," Susan says. "You did the right thing leaving New York. You just got off to a bumpy start. You'll be in a better place in a month."

I really hope she's right.

STICK SEASON

If Only I Had Known

Susan's text arrives on a blustery evening when I'm lying on the couch downstairs, a glass of red wine in hand. Ronan's head is propped up on a pillow that says *Good Boy*.

If you're coming upstairs to hang out with us tonight, you need to shower. We have company. Someone's coming to pick up one of Rooney's puppies. He told me he's in military intelligence! Better behave, or he might kidnap you!

Rooney's ten puppies are finally departing for their new homes. I've spent so much time upstairs playing with them in the whelping box. How will I let go of them? What am I going to do with my life when they leave?

Can't we just keep all of them?

No! They need to go off into the world and poop for other people.

I arrive upstairs just in time to meet a brawny guy with a sleeve tattoo and dirty-blond hair. He looks strange in Susan's living room. Maybe it's because of how tall he is. He makes a barstool's legs look like toothpicks.

Usually, Susan's puppy people are older couples from New England with flush retirement accounts, second homes, and empty-nest syndrome. The men wear polo shirts and Nantucket Reds and like to go sailing. Sometimes, there are outliers, younger couples from the city like me and Jack who show up wanting a puppy because they think it's going to fix everything, but rarely does a man arrive without anyone else in tow, especially one who looks like he could bench-press a hundred puppies. If Mr. Special Operations is married with kids, like Susan said a few days ago, where are they, and why isn't Susan asking more questions?

"So, you did the drive alone?" I ask. "Aren't you married?"

Susan shoots me a look. I can't help it! Someone's got to look out for these puppies.

Jack and I came together on adoption day. We even made a night of it and stayed at a hotel in town, the same one that I drive by all the time now and think, *Wow, if only I had known.*

"My family is back home in Virginia," Special Ops says. "It's a long drive, and it's a weeknight."

Good answer, I guess. I think I'm just expecting him to at least take his coat off and hang out for a bit. This isn't something to rush through. Ask questions. Doesn't he understand that this puppy is going to upend his life? Who keeps the dog if you get divorced?

"Do you want to sit down while I go get your puppy?" Susan asks.

The puppy you are going to use on your military intelligence missions?? I imagine one of Susan's puppies being used to sniff out terrorists or drugs. Ronan couldn't even catch a mouse. Maybe Susan should've put that in her contract as strictly forbidden.

"I'm fine standing," Special Ops says, sliding his hands into the pockets of his jeans. "I've been driving for hours."

"How about something to drink?" Jake asks.

Special Ops glances around the room. "Actually, I need to run outside and make a quick phone call." He darts down the stairs.

I wait until the front door closes. Something doesn't seem right. "Why does he need to go outside? Why can't he make his phone call in front of us? You can't tell me that either of you honestly trust this man. He hasn't smiled once, and he's about to go home with the cutest puppy in the world!"

"You just want to keep the puppy."

Fair point. "Did you screen him?"

Susan scoffs. "Are you kidding me? Of course I did. Don't you remember the rigamarole I put you through?"

"Of course I do. I have serious PTSD from that experience."

I talked to Susan for at least an hour on the phone, or rather, I spent an hour answering all her questions, proving I was worthy of being a puppy parent. Were dogs allowed in our apartment building? Had I ever owned a dog before? And then, the question to end all questions: "Do you have kids?"

"Why does that matter?" I replied.

"Some dogs aren't good with kids. Have you thought about that? Are you planning on having them?"

I wanted a dog, not a therapy session, and yet, she had asked the same question that I couldn't stop thinking about.

"We just got married. We want time to have it be . . . you know, just us."

Truthfully, it felt like we were running out of time. We had talked about kids in the beginning when we started dating but were nowhere closer to actually having them, even after a year of marriage. Jack was prioritizing work, and all I could think about was domestic life, raising an animal or a little human.

"Well, don't worry if you decide you want them. Glens are great with kids!"

It was as if I were on one of the many game shows I loved when I was a kid, where one wrong answer would disqualify me from winning Ronan. Thank God I passed. But what if I hadn't? Where would I be then? Definitely not here putting Special Ops through the same rite of passage.

The downstairs door opens again. "Shush!" Susan says. "He's coming back."

The dogs rush off to the landing. I pretend to zip my lips.

"I mean it!" she whispers.

Special Ops arrives back in Susan's living room, a little out of breath. His cheeks are rosy from the cool evening air. "What?" Maybe he needs to work more on his cardio.

"Nothing," Susan says. "Nothing at all. Let's get going here so you can get back on the road."

"You guys think I'm going to kill you, don't you?" Special Ops asks.

Wow. This puppy pickup is going worse than mine did, when Susan yelled at me for using my flip-flops to play tug of war with Ronan.

I lean back onto the couch. "We did, actually."

"Oh, come on. I was just kidding!" Special Ops rubs his hands together. "So, where is the little guy? I can't wait to meet him."

"He's a cute one," Jake says, over in the corner, zoning out in his favorite black chair. He says that about every puppy. He must have seen this song and dance a million times by now. He's just dreaming of the moment when Special Ops walks out the door so that he can make a martini with his new bottle of Kirkland vodka. Maybe I'll have him make me one tonight.

Susan returns to the living room with a squirming wheaten puppy in her arms and places him on a grooming table that she's set up in advance of this visit. Poor Susan. She tries to teach her puppy people how to groom correctly but hasn't yet realized that they all go home and make an appointment with a groomer and then end up divorced.

"Do you have a name picked out yet?" she asks.

"We were thinking about Finley."

"Finley! Lovely!"

"What's his registered A.K.C. name?" I ask. All of Susan's litters have a theme. She's done U2 songs, memoirs, places in Ireland, riffs on the word *love*. The official name for the dog they kept from their Pink Floyd litter was called *Another Brick in the Wall*. Ronan is Kilkenny's Granite Glen Ronan because his litter was their first in New Hampshire, the granite state.

"Finley will be known as Canis Major," Susan says. That's a good one. Latin for *the greater dog*.

Each time Finley sits his round furry behind on the table, Susan scoops her hand under his rear end and props him back up, then demonstrates a few grooming tips. I was just as overwhelmed the day I got my first grooming lesson from Susan. Now she does my grooming for me. She can't bear to look at a shaggy Glen. At least that's a bonus.

Poor Special Ops, though. He thought he was coming here to get a dog and is now staring at me on the couch, wondering where he went wrong. I'm just grateful he hasn't asked how I ended up back here with my dog.

"I'll stop," Susan says. "I don't want to overwhelm you, but before you leave, we need to take a photo."

Ah, yes. The all-important photo. Susan makes people pose with their puppy before walking out the door. Jack and I took a few shots in Susan's backyard (now *my* backyard), laughing, as we passed Ronan back and forth to each other. My favorite photo in the bunch is of little Ronan kissing me on the cheek.

Special Ops poses for his photo, then glances at the clock on the wall in Susan's kitchen. "Well, I should probably get going. I'm driving back tonight."

"Oh, sure. Well, of course. Drive safely. Nice to meet you. Let me know if you have any—"

Special Ops is already out the door. That took all of fifteen minutes. I press my nose to the front window, watching the taillights of his car pull out of the driveway, then disappear into the night. Farewell, Finley. I will miss you.

"He actually brought up killing us!" I yell. "That isn't something you joke about with strangers."

Susan plops herself into her favorite red chair. "It'll be fine. It was a joke. And he left just in time for us to watch *Jeopardy!*. Jake, pass me the remote and the vape. I'm feeling lucky tonight."

Lucky. That's how I hope Special Ops felt walking out of Susan's house. I've always felt that way about Ronan. Best thing I got out of my divorce.

Rooney jumps onto the couch and rolls over onto her back to give me easy access to her stomach. She has a twinkle in her eyes that says, *Thank God, one less baby hanging on my tits.*

I rub a spot behind her left ear, wishing that I didn't feel so badly about another puppy leaving the house, that I didn't have such severe attachment issues. But something just doesn't feel right. If Susan misread me and Jack, whose marriage was on the verge of collapse the day we showed up, what else is she wrong about?

"I think you made a huge mistake," I say. "You gave a puppy to a killer!"

Jake takes a hit off the vape, then passes it to Susan. "Here you go, dear. Maybe Betsy should have a couple hits tonight."

"Actually, can you make me a martini?" I ask.

"Everyone needs to relax. I know what I'm doing," Susan says.

It turned out she actually did. Not long after Special Ops visited, a friend request popped up for Ronan on his Instagram account from @finley_the_terrier. I flipped through photo after photo, unable to believe my eyes. Finley was living the dream down in Virginia: long walks on the beach, trips to Home Depot, wild runs through the sprinkler, a kiddie pool to play in, and a necklace that said "Boss."

I guess that makes Ronan Canis Minor.

How to Pick a Dildo

I wasn't quite sure what to expect when Susan invited me to a dinner party upstairs, but I hadn't ever thought that Jake would take his shirt off in the living room in front of the group to show off his new pacemaker. I can't recall ever seeing a seventy-something-year-old man without his shirt on, but I guess there's a first time in New England for everything.

Susan buries her forehead in her hands. "What am I going to do with you?"

A svelte woman named Patty who's dressed head to toe in black leans in and presses her index finger against Jake's chest.

"I can feel it in there! It feels hard!" she yells.

It's not even eight o'clock, and they're already getting naked. While it is cozy in here, with a roaring fire and Susan's dogs at my feet, I don't want to be next. Normally, I'd do an Irish goodbye, but they will definitely notice if I say I'm going to the bathroom and don't come back. I should go now before Susan gets out the board games.

"Well, I think that's it for me tonight," I say. "I've already eaten my share of your snacks."

"Nonsense!" Susan yells. "It's still early. Betsy, why don't you take the ladies downstairs? Show us your apartment and your vibrator!"

This night is just getting weirder. Even for Susan, this seems a bit shocking, especially since she was the one who told me to put my vibrator away before company arrived. Then again, Susan has been fascinated with it ever since I told her that I had one. I assumed she owned one, but she said that she "had Jake for that." I know she's not going to take no for an answer.

"Okay, ladies. Follow me!"

This is the first time since moving here that I've had guests in my apartment, and it feels kind of exciting, even if they're Susan's friends and not mine.

"Be careful," Susan says as we approach the stairs. "It can be slippery, and I don't want any of you suing me."

Susan flips on the golden teardrop light fixtures that dangle from the ceiling, still original from the '60s. We lumber down the narrow spiral staircase, one of my favorite features of Susan's house, the bridge between my world and hers.

Everyone shuffles into my apartment. Ronan rushes to the door to greet them.

"Oooooo, cozy!" Patty says.

It is. I love my apartment. Susan is great at decorating. It's just the way I'd design my house if I had taste and money. It's got a bohemian-chic vibe, cozy but funky, with a bathroom door painted marine blue and thick wooden shelves to support all my glasses. Colorful warm paintings and pictures dangle from the walls, lit by the warm glow of mismatched lamps and lampshades.

Susan points out the sea-green cabinets, subway kitchen tile, and new bathroom floor. Is she going to ask the ladies to check out the showerhead, like she asked me to do when I first moved in? Back then when she was giving me a house tour, she turned on the showerhead and flipped through multiple jet settings. The water dripped out in a slow misty spray, then fast into a full body power spray with a twist of the nozzle. She demonstrated a few more settings, spraying the shower curtain by accident.

"Jake told me to get the cheaper one, but I upgraded for you," she said.

A little puddle of water formed on the floor. "Oh, thanks. I hope it wasn't too expensive."

"What kind of setting do you like?"

I hadn't really ever thought about it. "My last bathroom in Brooklyn wasn't very nice. I never took baths. I didn't even have a plug for the tub."

"Well, hopefully this is an upgrade from the big city! I mean, you're single now, so you'll probably want a good showerhead right?"

"Why does being single matter?"

"You know ... for when you want to play around." She winked.

"Oh my God, I can't believe you said that."

"Why? What's wrong with getting off?"

"Nothing! But I use my vibrator for that."

Now she'll get to see it for the first time. I emerge back into the living room with my vibrator. I never thought I'd depend on it as much as I do, but I also never thought I'd be here explaining how it works to Susan and her friends, who are twenty-plus years older than me and hovering nearby with their martini glasses to catch a glimpse of my mysterious vibrator.

"Maybe I should get one," Susan says, sitting down onto my couch. "I'd never need Jake again."

"It's great! It makes being alone a lot more fun," I say.

"Weird. It's shaped like a thumb," another woman named Mary says. She's had way too many martinis tonight.

"Where do you put the batteries?" Patty asks, leaning in. "Isn't it supposed to look like a penis?"

Funny, I asked that exact question to a saleswoman at a sex store in Brooklyn the day I bought it, when the Moon Squad took me to buy a vibrator just before I left the city. We wandered in on a hot weekend afternoon and browsed handcuffs, whips, and paddles for sale. Bottles of lube and massage oil lined the shelves. Jars were filled to the brim with condoms. *Buy 12 get one free!*

I blame the priest who taught me about sex, but I have never felt fully comfortable in a sex shop. However, I did appreciate the step-by-step instructions for newbies on a sign that said: HOW TO PICK A DILDO.

For a decade, I had been using a Brookstone neck massager as my vibrator, and it worked just fine. Well, not all the time. Sometimes, the batteries ran out, or fell out, always at the most inconvenient time.

I picked up one of the vibrators on display, shaped like little bunny ears. Annie picked up a different model, turned it on, and pressed it against the back of my hand. "You're going to need to upgrade the shit you have if you're going off to live in the woods."

Even outside the office, project manager Annie was still trying to organize my life.

"She's right," Bridget said, while half-reading the back of a package of butt plugs. "Don't say I didn't warn you about New England winters. Are you sure you want to do this?"

I couldn't have been more certain that my time in the Empire State was up. I got annoyed every time I set foot on the subway. My divorce was finalized, and I had already quit my job. Hanging out with Bridget, Annie, and Sarah always made my decision to move so much more apparent. They still loved the city in ways I no longer did.

"I'm from Ohio! I can handle the winter," I said. "How much worse could it be?"

"Listen, New England is no joke," Bridget said. "I spent half my life there. You need a reliable model that will last in a snowstorm. You can't be jetting off to CVS in two feet of snow to buy batteries. How in the hell have you actually been getting off with a neck massager?"

"It got me through so many dry spells!" I yelled, attracting the attention of another salesgirl with an eyebrow ring.

My Brookstone only had two options—slow and fast—but it was a gift from a college friend who had one of her own. The device took two AA batteries. It was old-fashioned but incredible. I kept it under my pillow for easy access, and I passed on the joy and bought one for another friend who loved it so much that she sent me flowers as a thank-you.

What actually worried me more than making sure I picked the right vibrator was making friends after I left New York. Not having a full-time job lined up would make it harder to meet people. Would I find women in New England like me? Women who liked to get off and go to astrology readings and moon ceremonies?

Bridget picked up a vibrator that looked like a succulent. "Have you heard of JimmyJane? Top of the line."

I hadn't. As much as I wanted to be the big sister, setting a good example for my younger friends, they were frequently the ones educating me: on music, jumpsuits, hair color, and financial-planning strategies. I trusted all of their opinions. Whenever I listened to them, I always felt smarter and a little cooler.

"You'll never want another man in your life again if you get a JimmyJane," Annie said. "And quite honestly, I don't know how you'd want one anyway. Women are far superior."

"Well, that's good because I might not ever have one." I squinted at the small price tag. *$150?!*

JimmyJane was apparently the best of the best, so if I was going to splurge on a little self-care for my vagina, I should do it right. But how would I ever settle on a design and a color? I'd definitely have to keep it away from Ronan at that price. No hiding it under my pillow.

"Where do you put the batteries?" I flipped the vibrator upside down (or maybe it was right side up). Who could tell?

Annie laughed. "You plug it into your computer. USB."

"Convenient! It can charge while I'm working!"

I walked out of the sex shop that day with more credit card debt but hoped it would be worth it. I didn't have snow boots, snow tires, a down jacket, or even a car, but that day I left New York, I had my new vibrator tucked away in my duffel bag.

Looking back now, I can't think of a smarter purchase I made. The first month in New Hampshire ended up being tougher than I expected. I barely knew anyone other than Susan and the salespeople at King Arthur Bakery. The Moon Squad was right—I needed my JimmyJane to survive. At night, I'd get under the covers and gaze out my window, the dead autumn leaves swirling around in the wind. It was so easy for my loneliness to drag me down into a dark place, but my vibrator never let me down. All I had to do was press a button to escape real life.

Now, I get to demonstrate how it works. I hand my vibrator to Patty and try to not think about all the other places it's been, kind of like when Ronan licks his balls, then my face, seconds later.

"How many batteries does it take?" Patty asks.

"It doesn't. It's USB-powered," I say to confused stares. "That means it plugs right into my computer. Work first, play later."

Ronan jumps onto the couch and leans against the armrest. "What does Ronan do when you use it?" Susan asks. "Doesn't he sleep with you?"

"He flies off the bed faster than you can say, 'JimmyJane.'"

"How do you put it up inside you?" Patty asks.

Up inside you? "It's for outside use only. Well, I guess maybe you could, but it's kind of wide. Do you have lube?"

Patty hands the vibrator back to me. "Show me."

Does she want me to take off my pants? I press a tiny button on the front. "This setting is pretty great. It pulses like a wave." I tap my vibrator against Patty's hand so she can feel it. "Don't worry, I wash it after every use."

I finish off the show by demonstrating the vibrator's fastest setting. "This one is my favorite. It makes you forget your problems pretty fast."

"Just what I need!" Susan says.

Guess I know what I'll be getting her for Mother's Day.

Winter Is Coming

A line is already snaking out the door of the tire shop by the time I arrive, just like a popular bakery in New York City but without the benefit of actual carbohydrates. Maybe I should have gotten up earlier. This would be a lot more fun with mimosas. I tap the shoulder of the man in front of me.

"Am I getting in today for my snow tires? This is my first time here, and the line is pretty long."

"Oh, you'll get your snows done today—don't worry. But those people won't," he replies in a half-snicker, pointing to the unfortunate people in line behind us wearing light jackets and Dartmouth windbreakers.

It's November. Susan has been pestering me to put on my snow tires for the last month, but I've been too lazy and skeptical to budge. I don't drive a lot, and I don't want to pay $100 for something I don't need.

"Go now, before it gets too busy!" she's said nearly every time I've seen her.

Susan sounds a lot like my mother, who was ten minutes early for everything. In this way, I am nothing like my mother. I have always been a procrastinator, someone who believes she can bend time to her wishes. I hadn't thought much about the change in season, even though most of the leaves have floated off the trees. I've overheard locals at the grocery store talk about the pending change of season in hushed tones: "Winter is coming," as if we are all extras on *Game of Thrones*. It seems really hard to believe that the weather will shift soon.

"What's your license plate number?" a mechanic asks when I finally arrive at the counter, his pants covered in streaks of grease.

I actually don't know. I've only been driving the car for a month.

"It's a Toyota, the oldest car in the lot with bumper stickers all over the back. You can't miss it. Well, actually maybe you will. I've wedged it in between two giant SUVs."

"What's your name?"

"Elizabeth," I say, dropping my car keys on the counter. That's the name I use when doing business.

"That's it for today," the mechanic yells to the rest of the line. "I'm sorry, but the rest of you will have to go home."

Groans fill the room. "This is bullshit!" someone yells, storming off. The door snaps shut behind him.

I made it in the nick of time. Only one empty seat was left in the waiting room. Snow tires, like death and jury duty, are the ultimate equalizer. Everyone needs them. A budding journalist, sitting to my left, works for public radio and is one of the first to get dismissed.

"Everything looks super. It's obviously brand new," a mechanic tells her.

This is something he's absolutely not going to say about my car. The car is fifteen years old. Who knows the last time the brakes were repaired or the last time it got a new battery? I hope no one scams me into getting work done.

Bridget, a Boston native, warned me about New England winters before I moved to Hanover, but in Ohio we had below-zero temperatures all the time, and we never drove around with snow tires. I remember listening to the radio with my mother, praying that school would be canceled. Oh, the disappointment I felt when public schools were closed, but our Catholic school just up the road was open. Did the nuns think that Jesus would help us get to school? Or that if we died in a car accident, our souls would be saved? Or maybe it was more about getting that long summer they felt they so deserved, lounging outside, sipping their dirty martinis made with Baptism water. How badly I wanted to stay home back then, but I can't do that now. I need to be able to get to the grocery store for pretzels and Cabot spreadable cheddar cheese for dipping purposes.

"Elizabeth?"

Here it comes. My car is ready. I rise to receive my sentencing. The mechanic hands over the keys but doesn't offer any additional services. He doesn't even tell me to get an entirely new car.

"You had my Toyota, right?" I ask. "The 2002 one? With a large dent on the right-hand side and rust by the back left wheel? Barely running?"

"That's the one. Snow tires in the trunk?"

Weird. But who am I to argue with good news? Maybe I worried for nothing. I hand over my credit card and putter away from the tire shop, wondering if I'll be able to sense the difference with my snow tires on, and boy do I ever. My car won't stop yanking to the right. It's barely drivable. I pull into the first Dunkin' Donuts I see so that I can call the shop and complain with an egg-and-cheese breakfast sandwich in my hand.

"You'll have to bring it back tomorrow morning," a woman on the other end says. "We don't have time to do it today."

"But you ruined my car!"

"Tomorrow," she repeats, then hangs up.

If only I had brought Susan, my personal litigator, with me this time.

It's late afternoon when I arrive home and let Ronan out for a pee. An angry gust of wind tosses a pile of crunchy leaves across the yard. Ronan turns around and gives me a fearful look that says, *Winter is coming.* I feel it in the air too. When I moved to Hanover in the fall, I thought I had chosen the best time of year, with the gorgeous leaves at their peak, but it turns out my timing was awful. October in New England is the beginning of a long, slow descent into darkness.

Overnight, the first frost arrives, dusting the earth with delicate ice crystals. Ronan is even more tentative today. He normally takes his time doing his morning pee, but he quickly lifts a leg on the fence pole and whines to be let back in. I throw on some leggings and rush out the door. I don't have a scraper for my windshield, so I have to sit in my car with the defrosters on full blast, losing valuable time in the driveway, muttering every swear word I can think of.

The trees look beautiful now, frozen in ice, but I know the line at the car shop is going to be even worse today. Maybe I should have put on my snow tires weeks earlier, when Susan told me to, but that's the problem with time. You can't tell you've run out of it until it's too late.

I had been so skeptical of snow tires, and when I arrive back at the car shop, I finally realize why. I may be an outsider, but I hadn't been wrong to question the relevance of snow tires. The mechanic explains in very convoluted language that the snow tires were actually on my car all along. The first time I came in, the mechanic accidentally replaced them with the summer tires that were in my trunk.

"So, you mean to tell me that I didn't even need to come in here in the first place because the snow tires were already on my car and that I paid $100 for nothing?" I ask.

Neither Susan nor the mechanic realized it. That still doesn't quite explain why my alignment was off (story of my life), but hopefully, they'll figure that out today.

The mechanic takes my keys. "Have a seat, and we'll swap them back out for you."

I would, if only there were a place to sit.

Welcome to Farm-Way

I can't recall ever seeing this many pairs of boots in my life. The walls are lined with obscure brands I've never heard of, names harder to pronounce than prescription drugs. Oboz, Lowa, Dansko, Chaco. If I want to buy a canoe, kayak, snowshoes, Crocs, pigskin gloves, Adirondack chairs, hay, or farm supplies, I'm also in luck.

Susan sits down onto a bench. "Welcome to Farm-Way."

She insisted we come here to buy my first pair of boots, a rite of passage for newcomers. Farm-Way is in Vermont, just over the New Hampshire border.

"If you want to look for coats too . . ."

"There's more?"

"There's a second floor!"

I lean against a wooden pillar and take in the taxidermic deer head above me on the walls. "This feels like the last place a vegetarian should shop."

"That will absolutely not get you a discount around here."

I hope I find boots today that I like. I could use retail therapy more than ever. The leaves have fallen off the trees, scattered in heaps on the ground, leaving bare branches that look like skeleton limbs. We're living in the in-between, the time between autumn and winter. Stick season, the locals call it. I love this about New England, that there's a name for every season, for everything you're feeling. I wish there had been a better name for the in-between period between married and divorced. *Separated* just doesn't have a good ring to it, whereas stick season fits perfectly. It feels like I've been stripped down to the bone too.

"Can I help you with something?" a saleswoman asks, popping out from behind a sales rack. She eyes my gray Converse sneakers. I wore these all the time when I still lived in the city. I love them, but they're not going to cut it in winter.

"I'm looking for boots."

"What kind? Muck boots?"

Muck boots? What are those? Is that what I'm supposed to be wearing this time of year? "Do you carry Patagonia?" That's the only brand I know.

She laughs. "Honey, half our store is Patagonia. I'll give you a minute to look around."

She seems eager. I suppose that makes sense. There are hardly any customers in here. Strange.

"Where are all the people?" I ask Susan, who's sticking her foot into a pair of furry UGGs that look like the pair she wore when she took me to my job interview.

"They're all gone. Foliage season is over."

At least I don't have to fight off a crowd right now. I feel tired, and I haven't even tried anything on yet. Maybe I should treat this boot-shopping experience the way I shop for magical crystals—just see what calls to me. Thank God I haven't given up sessions with my astrologer. We do trades now, where she gives me free sessions and, in return, I write and edit her website. The last time we talked, she told me that Jupiter, the planet of luck and blessings, was transiting my fifth house, a good sign for romance. I hope she's right.

Susan points to a rugged pair of ankle boots. "How about those? HOKAs. That's all Jake and I wear in the winter."

That makes me think of what Jake always says: "There's no bad weather in New England, just bad clothes." I guess HOKAs are appropriate for the season. They look like boots for hiking, something I don't do.

"Are they on sale?"

I could be swayed for a bargain. My mother loved the sales section. Nothing made her happier than getting something for half price. I imagine how the two of us would tackle this store; we'd split off to explore, then return to each other with what we found.

The boots that Susan has picked up are $150. I guess I could put them on my credit card, but I'm trying to improve my credit score, not destroy it. One thing I've found so far is that I'm spending less money here. I can go without all the things I blew my money on in the city, the things that brought me temporary joy—balayage hair color, spinning classes, facials, and mani-pedis—though now in this moment, I wish my mother were here to put my new boots on *her* credit card.

I pick up the HOKA boots and run my fingers over their grippy soles. "I don't know . . . turquoise laces?" I'll let Susan tell me what to do when it comes to Ronan, but I think I can handle buying my own shoes. "It looks like they glow in the dark."

"That means cars will see you on the street when you're walking Ronan. It's getting darker earlier now . . ."

She's right. Ever since we turned the clocks back an hour, night falls around 4:30. The lights are always on in New York City, and I cannot get over how dark it is here. I start winding down for the night not long after dinner and fall asleep around nine. Maybe it's the absence of light, but life feels more hopeless than usual right now. Winter is coming, and there's nothing I can do about it other than prepare. I have an ice scraper, vitamin D pills, and drugstore face masks. I need boots, too, but not these. "I don't like how they look."

"They're waterproof, and they'll keep you dry in the winter. Try them on!"

I want something that looks like me, although truthfully, I don't really know what my style is anymore.

When I first moved to New York City, I went to Bloomingdale's to buy boots for work. I wanted something comfortable that I could walk for blocks in but trendy enough that I could wear them on dates. I ended up with pull-on, knee-high boots, then brought them back a few days later for a different pair with zippers up the back. I still have them ten years later, but I won't be able to walk Ronan in them when there's a foot of snow on the ground. I knew what I was giving up when I left the city, but I hadn't thought that I'd need a new wardrobe too. I'm glad Susan is here helping me. I would've never known about Farm-Way if it weren't for her. She's lived in Vermont and New Hampshire for half her life. Maybe I should listen to her. She probably knows what she's talking about.

"I'm going to look around a little more," I say. "But let's add these to the maybe column."

"Well, no matter what boots you get, you'll need a pair of these." She swipes a pair of purple-and-pink wool socks off a rack. "What's your shoe size?"

"Seven."

"I'm a seven and a half."

My mother was a seven and a half. Doesn't sound like much of a difference, but her shoes were still a smidge too big for me. When I was going through her closet after her death, sorting her clothes for Goodwill, I wanted to keep so many of her shoes but couldn't because they fell off my feet when I tried to walk in them.

"Darn Tough socks," Susan says. "Everyone wears that brand here, even Bernie Sanders. You need a pair. They'll last forever."

"Nothing lasts forever, especially socks."

"They do! I have pairs from years ago, and I still wear them."

The price tag catches my eye. Twenty-five bucks for socks? They better last forever.

But there's still the matter of boots. I can't leave today without a pair. I roam the aisles, my eyes tracing rows and rows of rugged brown and black boots that actually just look like variations on each other. Maybe I should have done this online. That probably would have been a lot easier. I turn a corner and spot a pair of Merrell brown boots with white fur on the top that looks like whimsical fluff. There's something about them that I like, a mix of sensible and fashionable. I ask for a seven and plop myself onto the bench next to Susan.

"So, no HOKAs?" she asks. "And what about the fur? You're a vegetarian . . ."

"I like the fur. It's fun. And it's fake!"

I slip my right foot into one boot, then run my fingers along the bottom of the boots. They feel grippy, like they'd be able to handle snow and ice. I hope Ronan doesn't mistake the fur on them for a chew toy.

"Make sure you walk in them a little before you buy them," Susan says.

Good advice. I tie my laces, then strut up and down an aisle, imagining a snowy morning with Ronan at my side, walking around the neighborhood. The boots are so comfortable that it feels like they're hugging my feet. I don't know what winter will bring, but at least I feel ready for it now.

"I really love these. Do you think they would let me wear them out of the store?"

Susan hands me the empty box. "This is Vermont. You can do whatever the fuck you want."

WHISKEY SEASON

Stud Dog at Your Service

Susan mutes the television during a *Jeopardy!* commercial break. "I think I might have someone for Ronan, a lady friend."

"A lady friend?" I prop myself up on the couch next to Picabo. She paws at me for a head rub.

Jake slides an olive off the toothpick in his chilled martini glass. "For sex."

"For puppies!" Susan says.

Am I hearing her right? That she wants to use Ronan as a stud dog? When Jack and I got Ronan as a puppy, Susan had asked if we'd consider keeping Ronan's balls to breed him one day. We said okay. Who doesn't love puppies? Then again, I hadn't ever thought "one day" might actually happen.

"Hand me my iPad," she says, putting on her glasses. It feels like we're cruising a dating app with all the photo swiping she's doing. She spins her iPad around to show me the screen, a photo of a little gray dog. "Cute, right? Do you think Ronan would be into it?"

If only she knew all the inanimate objects Ronan has wrapped his legs around: my teddy bears and pillows, the armrest of my old couch. I don't know what Ronan's type is, but I assume it is a lot like mine right now: anything with a pulse. I'm a little bit worried, though, about this small and dainty girl. Will Ronan's forty-seven pounds of very good boy enthusiasm be too much for her?

"Her name is Confidence," Susan says.

"Confidence? This is the weirdest conversation we've ever had, and we've had a lot of weird conversations."

"Don't you want Ronan to get his rocks off?" Jake asks, taking the last sip of his martini.

"He'd make really nice puppies!" Susan says. "He's got the best head on a Glen I've ever seen. All we need to do is run some genetic tests and make sure he's healthy enough to tango."

"What kind of tests?"

"He needs his hips done. X-rays."

I don't like the sound of it. All the preparation reminds me of my efforts to freeze my eggs, the $10,000 price tag for bloodwork and hormone medications, just to get four eggs that are now chilling on ice somewhere in New Jersey.

"Do you think pet insurance would cover it?" I ask. "I doubt they'd cover sex expenses, but I guess I could always try."

"So, you're in?"

Am I in? Of course I am. Ronan has been waiting his whole life for this, and I can't think of anything better than holding one of his puppies. I want only the best for him but not before I get the chance to have sex in this house.

"Would you want to keep a puppy?" Susan asks.

"Maybe. I'd really love a girl. What else does this entail, exactly, aside from a trip to the vet?"

"I need you to send me cute pictures of Ronan."

"Why? Are you going to send them to Confidence to see if she's into it?"

"You'll see."

"It's his first time. What if he can't get it up?"

Susan whips off her glasses. "Don't worry. I'm great with a turkey baster!"

The next few weeks are a whirlwind of preparation. Susan relishes the opportunity to put her lawyer skills to work and draws up a contract, an agreement for stud services that has Ronan's photo on it. I picked the best photo of him I could find, where it looks like he's actually smiling. Per Susan's request, I bought K-Y Jelly from the grocery store, just in case.

When we get word that Confidence is ovulating, we drive to

Massachusetts to get her, then bring her back to the house. "Where should we introduce them?" I ask.

"Let's put her in the backyard for now," Susan says.

Jake opens the back gate to let us in but doesn't close it fast enough. Confidence dashes out and races off down the driveway. Susan hops in her car. "Come on, we've gotta catch her!"

Jake and I take off on foot. "Divide and conquer," he says. "You go that way. Ask the neighbors if they've seen anything."

I start with the next-door neighbor. It occurs to me that I've been in this driveway before. It's the same one that Jack and I pulled into when we picked Ronan up as a puppy. We drove past Susan's house by mistake and had to turn around. What if the owner had come out and warned us about his neighbors Susan and Jake "the crazy dog people" whose dogs barked all day long? Maybe we would've rethought everything and sped back to New York. Where would I be then?

Part of me is hoping that no one is home, but I'm out of luck. A bespectacled gray-haired man wearing a plaid shirt walks out of his garage before I even have the chance to knock on his door. "Can I help you?"

If you only knew, I think, trying to catch my breath. "I live next door with Susan and Jake. Your neighbors who have the RV in the driveway? I was wondering... have you seen a dog?"

He looks me up and down, then past me, perhaps looking for the secret camera that he thinks is filming him for a reality show.

"Gray little thing?" he says.

It can't be. "Yes!"

"She's out back in our cat pen!"

I cannot believe any of this. All along, I thought that Susan, Jake, and I were the weirdos on the block who organized dog sex parties, but it actually turns out that we pale in comparison to our neighbors. I follow the man around the back of the house to find an extraordinary sight—a web of netting suspended around trees and bushes. I spot Confidence right away, in a far-off corner. I call her over, pick her up, and carry her out the door.

"Been that kind of day," I say, passing a very confused neighbor.

"Thanks for your help!"

Back home, Susan and I put Confidence in the yard and sigh with relief. "Now what?" I ask.

"Let's put them together and see what happens. Go get your stud."

It takes me a second to register that my stud is Ronan, my angel pupper who kept me company and snuggled close to me all those lonely nights during my divorce, the same one whose baby teeth I saved, who I dressed up as the pope for Halloween, and who has professional portraits to mark his first birthday. I may not have children, but I have Ronan, who's about to celebrate his upcoming birthday in style, by losing his virginity.

I wish I could relax, the way I did when we got Ronan. I didn't care whether we were getting a boy or a girl. Susan didn't even tell us until a few days before we arrived that we were getting a boy. I just had this strange feeling that it would work out, no matter who we ended up with.

Back inside, I spot Ronan in my living room on his favorite club chair, his fluffy white elbow on the armrest. All that's missing is a cigar in his paw. "Ronan, I need to talk to you."

He flies off the chair and rushes out the open door, straight for the backyard. I don't even need to have a condom discussion. What I do need is alcohol. I pour two glasses of red wine, one for me and one for Susan. I arrive in the backyard just in time for the courtship. Susan rustles up an Adirondack chair to supervise.

"You brought wine?" she asks.

I hand Susan a glass. "Do you know how weird this is for me? To watch my dog have sex? He's my little boy, not a horny stud dog!"

"You don't have to watch!"

How do mothers of teenage boys deal with this kind of thing? I want to be here in case they run into trouble, not that I would know the first thing about how to save them, but it already appears like they have gotten off to a great start. Ronan and Confidence take turns chasing each other around the yard, leaving behind frisky pawprint tracks. Occasionally, they'll stop so that Ronan can lick her ears. He really does dwarf her in size. His paws are bigger. His head is bigger. His, well I don't want to think about that, is also bigger. They sprint back and forth under a hammock, finally stopping in a far-off corner of the yard. There's nowhere else to go, but they don't care. All they want is each other.

"Are they trying to get some privacy?" I ask. "Should we leave them alone?"

"No, we need to be here in case they need help. Maybe you should go get that lubricant."

I don't need to. In no time at all, Confidence and Ronan have somehow attached themselves to each other, their rear-ends touching. "Why are they standing like that?"

"It's a tie!" Susan yells. Susan and Jake high-five.

"A tie?"

"It's dog speak for doin' it," Jake says. "They attach to each other until the job is done. What did you expect?"

"I don't know. Something that looked more like actual sex?"

I had been so worried about little Confidence, but she seems like the one who's in control. After twenty minutes of being attached to each other (far longer than a lot of my sexual experiences) Confidence trots off, barely breaking a sweat, and waits at the door for one of us to let her inside. She's ready for dinner. Ronan is still panting. Today was the best day of his life, until tomorrow, when we get to do this all over again.

Susan plops herself down onto the chair. "I've been doing this for twenty years, and I don't think I ever had a stud dog get it up that fast."

Two months later, even better news arrives: Confidence has given birth to four puppies, all boys. Guess I'll have to keep waiting for my girl. I can't get over how Ronan and Confidence clicked like magic. No lube or turkey baster required. No $10,000 fertility treatment entrance fee. Ronan had better luck than I did. My little man is officially a stud.

I scour Instagram like a crazy ex-girlfriend, waiting in the shadows for someone to post a photo of those puppies. I know one day it will come, and finally it does: A photo of a woman my age, smiling big, cross-legged on the floor, with one very familiar looking gray puppy in her lap. The Dumbo ears, the dark nose, the kissable paws. He is unmistakable. He's Ronan's son, out there in the world, a good boy making someone happy. That's all that really matters . . . and that he has a solid Irish name. Quigley.

A Very Marijuana Christmas

Susan slides a heavy, square-shaped item into my hands wrapped in Wednesday's edition of the newspaper. She's bundled up in a warm sweater and black leggings. "We don't believe in wrapping paper."

It's Christmas morning, and there's a roaring fire in the living room. Anytime a fire is lit, it feels special. It snowed last night, and the world outside feels soft. Susan and Jake's kids, Joe and Jackson, have come home from New York and California. What do they think of me being here? The tenant wearing mismatched wool socks, who's living downstairs, where they usually sleep when they come home. There's already been one argument about how cold it is in the RV, where Joe is sleeping.

I had every intention of leaving Susan's house for Christmas, a holiday that has been terrible for me practically every year since my mother died. The last few years, I've spent it with friends. This year wouldn't be any easier, now that I'm alone and divorced. I thought about running off somewhere but wasn't sure where to go. Ireland maybe? I decided to stay once Susan told me everything she planned to cook.

"I'm making cheesy scalloped potatoes!" she said. "You'll love them!"

How could I say no?

"Hopefully, there won't be blood on them this time," she said. A few years ago, Jake sliced a finger on the mandolin, which earned him a trip to the hospital and stitches for Christmas.

So far this morning, I've had a couple pastries from King Arthur

Bakery, and I plan on eating everything Susan puts in front of me.

"Go on, open your present!" she says.

I rip open my present, nearly knocking over my champagne glass. Newspaper flies onto the floor. Picabo lunges for it, as if it's a Frisbee.

"A cookbook?"

"That's right. Eat healthy. No more frozen pizza! I'm gluten-free, and I can smell you making it downstairs every night."

It's really hard to believe that the smell of my pizza would travel all the way upstairs, but I guess I can hear them playing *Jeopardy!* after all.

"I have something for you," I say, handing Susan her Christmas present.

She shakes the box. "Wow! Real wrapping paper! You must really love me. Hmm . . . I wonder what this is?" I think she already knows. She unwraps the gift, then holds it up for everyone to see. "Hair spray!"

A few weeks ago, Susan ran out of hair spray, so I lent her mine. She loved how it smelled. Hair spray always makes me think of my mother, how she did her hair every morning without fail. By the time I came down for breakfast to eat my Lucky Charms, I could smell the hair spray floating into the kitchen from the bathroom.

I flip through a few pages of my new cookbook, remembering the Strawberry Shortcake plates and make-believe vacuum that my parents got me for Christmas and how neither did much to turn me on to domestic life. The recipes look kind of complicated. Maybe I can just convince Susan to make them for me.

"Were those Greta sugar cookies you made the other night gluten-free?" I ask.

I had found Susan in her kitchen wearing a pink pussy hat. The refrigerator door was ajar, and all the dogs had positioned themselves around the flour-covered counter, tongues out. They thumped their tails against the floor when they saw me. I bent over to give Rooney some snuggles. Outside the window, snow fell.

"Oh, good, it's you," she said.

"Who else would it be?"

"Can you try out my cookies? I'm too stoned."

I guess when you're a retired cancer survivor, having a little smoke in the afternoon for the holidays is perfectly acceptable. "Is there pot in them?"

"Never. I don't mix my drugs with my desserts."

Still, Susan must have been the perfect amount of high because the cookies were covered in sprinkles and were absolute perfection. I popped one in my mouth. It was so soft that it melted on my tongue. "Oh my God."

"Shit. Are they bad?"

I reached for another. "They're incredible."

With their crispy crust and spongy center, the cookies were far too good to share with the dogs, but when Susan wasn't looking, I let them lick my fingers.

Now, the Gretas are on the counter, but we aren't allowed to have any until later. Torture. Rooney jumps up next to me on the couch and places her head in my lap. Everyone is in good spirits, especially Susan, who loves the holidays. She loves food and alcohol and her kids and her mom, who's coming over later.

She picks up the champagne bottle and motions for my glass. "You seem a little sad. Are you okay? Have more champagne."

I don't need to be told twice. I hope I'm not a downer for everyone. I just wish that my mother was around to make Christmas special. Thinking back to the holidays in my house, I don't remember my parents being huge drinkers in my childhood, but Christmas brought out a whole new side of them.

"Where's our highballs?" my godparents asked when they showed up, pushing their way through a spiderweb of garland and all the other decorations my mother plastered to the back door.

"On it!" my mother yelled back, wearing a Christmas sweater and a Santa pin, her dexterous hands whipping up cocktails to numb the pain of screaming children and fingers that hurt from hours of gift-wrapping. We'd be going to Mass in a couple of hours, and no one in their right mind wanted to do that sober.

I didn't know what was in a highball, but I knew I wasn't allowed to have it. Not wanting to leave out the children, my mother made a virgin sherbet punch that we could enjoy in little cups while we pretended to be good little drinkers just like our parents. It never occurred to me back then that there would come a day when all that would end. You always think you have more time than you really do.

My mother loved Christmas so much that we decided to play Mannheim Steamroller's Christmas album at her wake, even though she died in October. Christmas that year was terrible. No one put up decorations or holiday lights. No one strung popcorn and cranberries on the Christmas tree. No Nat King Cole on the record player, no stockings on the fireplace, no coffee in the percolator. No dog greeting me at the back door. My father gave her away and didn't tell me before I came home for the holiday. Maybe he didn't want the responsibility that comes with taking care of a dog. Maybe he didn't want any more reminders of my mother. Maybe he thought I wouldn't care, given that I was away at college. I just wish he would have told me beforehand, but communication has never been great in my family.

Now as I sit in Susan's living room, surrounded by a family intact, I wonder how my relationship would have turned out with my mother if she had lived. Would we share champagne, the way Susan and Jake pass the vape to Joe and Jackson?

"Hey, now, listen up," Jake says. "You kids can't get too stoned. We gotta go snow-blow the driveway. Betsy, you wanna help?"

Hell no. Every time I step onto the driveway, I'm taking my life in my hands. Just last week, Susan sent a frantic message in the morning asking me to shovel the end of the driveway. "I have to take Jake to a doctor's appointment, and the mailman needs to get in and out!"

If Susan could get out of the driveway, then why couldn't the mailman get in? No point in telling Susan I've never shoveled a driveway before. Surely, I will just have to go to YouTube for guidance, the way I did when I wanted some tips on raking leaves. Until Jake gets accustomed to his new pacemaker, he isn't allowed to do strenuous work. That means Susan and I have to run operations around the house, or rather, she runs operations, and I do all the actual running.

With the dogs' hopeful brown eyes watching me through the windows, fogging up the glass with their big tongues, I trudged out into the snow to the end of the driveway, shovel in hand. I had barely shoveled for five minutes when I slipped on a patch of ice and collapsed onto my back. Live free or die trying to shovel your driveway.

"I'm too scared of our driveway," I say now, propping my feet up on the coffee table. "I've fallen so many times." There's no way I'm leaving this house on Christmas Day.

"Please don't sue us," Susan says.

"She's not going to sue us," Jake says. "Falling means you're part of the family. I fall all the time."

"That's why you can't go out and shovel with your new pacemaker," Susan says.

"I don't have enough money to sue you," I say. "And you'd destroy me in court anyway."

Jake reaches for the bottle of champagne. "Sounds like we could all use a top-up."

I pass my glass to Susan. Joe takes a hit from the vape. We spend the rest of the morning playing board games and feeding the fire with logs of wood. I doze off on Susan's couch and wake up just in time to try the biggest cheeseball I've ever seen. Susan doesn't say that she made it, which means she got it at Costco. I like that Susan's rituals—the mandolin, gifts wrapped in newspaper, King Arthur pastries for breakfast—aren't the ones I grew up with. Nothing has triggered me or made me cry. Today has just felt like a lazy weekend morning.

All in all, it's been a good day. I call my father to wish him a happy Christmas. This year, he's going over to my godparents' house. Jake seems pleased with the bottle of liquor I bought him ("As long as it's gin, he won't give a shit," Susan instructed me beforehand), but I think he's more delighted with the state-of-the-art vape he got from the kids.

The sun sets by four o'clock. That's December in New England for you. The fire has mellowed to a soft sizzle. Jake and Joe lumber back into the living room, carrying more logs of wood to keep the fire going, dragging sloppy puddles of snow behind them. Esther, Susan's mom, will be arriving soon. I guess that means it's time for me to shower. The dogs toddle behind me to the landing, never daring to follow me down the stairs. "Don't worry, I'll be back," I tell them as their tails wag back and forth, like furry metronomes.

"Dinner is at six!" Susan calls out after me. "Don't be late! I have more wine and vegetarian stuff for you, and we're going to play Cards Against Humanity. But keep it clean. No swearing in front of my mom."

Rooney whines as I disappear down the staircase. "I'll be back, sweetie." By the time I reach the bottom of the stairs, Jake has finalized arrangements with the kids.

"Time to put away the pot," he says. "We gotta go get Grandma."

Are You a Leo?

"Tell me one word that sums up how you feel right now," my yoga teacher Maeve says, a sub whom I've never had before. Mala prayer beads dangle from her neck.

Shitty.

I can't say that aloud in this room, filled with a half dozen women, who look just like me, sitting cross-legged in their leggings and sports bras, waiting for class to begin. I'm wearing a tangerine quartz crystal around my neck to attract fun and playfulness into my life . . . still waiting for the crystal's power to kick in.

Maeve points to a woman in the front row, no doubt a college student. "How about you? What's your word?"

"Content."

Content? Content with a foot of snow on the ground? It's another blustery day, with dreary skies out the windows. Gray every damn day.

My turn is coming. How else am I feeling?

Hopeless. Can't say that either, but it's true.

"What about you in the back row?" Maeve asks.

The other women turn around to face me.

"I don't know. Lonely, I guess."

Less dramatic than *shitty* but still true.

"Lonely, wow . . ." Maeve says. "That's a hard one, but I've been there too. We've got a new moon coming up though. A great time to set new intentions."

Am I hearing her right? Did she just mention the moon? I haven't talked about astrology and the moon with anyone since leaving New

York and the Moon Squad. I wonder what her sign is. I love trying to guess people's astrological signs. I get so much joy when I guess correctly, as if I've come a step closer to figuring out who they really are. I think I have a good feeling about this woman, Maeve. She plays good music, and she's spunky. Looks just like Reese Witherspoon. She seems confident. Maybe an Aries? Or a Leo? Maybe I could ask her to grab a coffee? It seems simple enough—just ask if she wants to hang out—and yet I don't know what to say to her. It's as if I've completely forgotten how to make friends. I don't have a job where I have coworkers, and I'd rather die than join a ski club. Actually, I probably would die if I joined the ski club because I don't know how to ski. But I also haven't tried hard to make friends because I hadn't planned to stick around this long when I moved up here from New York City. Maybe I should've had a better plan. Five months later, I'm still here.

I thought I always had Susan and Jake to keep me company, but I'm not so sure anymore. The other night, we were out at an art event and ran into people Jake knew, friends of his kids who were my age.

"We're all going out to a party after this . . . why don't you come?" someone asked me.

I froze.

Jake elbowed me. "You should go. You're young! Go out and have fun! Stop hangin' out with us oldies."

"But I want to hang out with you. If we leave now, we can make it home in time for *Jeopardy!*."

"We like having you around, but we think you need to make some friends your own age," Susan said.

I know I need to start putting myself out there, but all I wanted that night was to snatch a few business cards, then go home with Susan and Jake and order Thai food. Making friends is a sign that I'm here to stay, and I'm not sure if that's the case.

While Maeve leads us through class, I try to remember how I made friends when I was a teenager. Funny how that was more than twenty years ago, but it still feels just as hard as it did when I turned fourteen and started attending a new Catholic high school across town. I didn't know anyone. All my friends went to public school. I came home and cried to my mother and begged her to let me transfer schools.

"Try and stick it out a little longer," she said. "See what happens . . . give it some time."

How long was I supposed to wait? I felt so impatient, but my mother had been right. Life eventually worked out. I just had to be patient. And yet now, I still feel unsure of how long I should stay in Hanover. I don't know if I have it in me to make it through another winter. Should I start looking for jobs on the West Coast? Get a job in Ireland as a sheepherder?

Maybe this year will fly by as fast as Maeve's yoga class. There's drippy condensation all over the windows by the time she dims the lights and leads us into final relaxation, my favorite part of class, where we get to close our eyes and do nothing. "Try spending this time thinking about what you're grateful for today."

Well, this will be a short list. What am I grateful for? Ronan, above everything. I can't imagine my life without him. He got me through my divorce, and I love the long walks we take around the neighborhood. And of course, I am thankful for Susan and Jake, who brought Ronan into the world and cook meals for me and serve cocktails when I wander upstairs feeling lonely. What else? I love how cozy my bedroom is, the way the morning sunlight sneaks in through the pine trees and casts fun shadows on my closet. Even though the closet doors are broken, it still looks pretty. I love how much freedom I have now, compared to my life in New York. It's the middle of the afternoon, and I'm in a yoga class. I couldn't ever do that before! I love how close I am to King Arthur Bakery. Maybe I'll go there after this and get a slice of pizza. Funny, now that I think about it, that's actually a fair amount of stuff. Maybe I should give life here a little more time. If I wait until October to make any decisions about what to do next, that would be a full year. That seems like a fair amount of time to see what happens. Maybe I'm where I'm supposed to be right now, just waiting and thinking.

At the end of class, we roll up our yoga mats, and I find Maeve at the front desk behind a computer. Now's my shot. She's my age, likes the moon and yoga. What more could I ask for in a friend? I just need to put myself out there.

I lean my yoga mat against the wall. "This might sound a little crazy, but I was trying to guess your astrological sign all class, and I have a pretty good track record, so I have to ask—are you a Leo?"

She laughs. "No, I'm a Gemini."

A Gemini! How about that. "You are? Me, too!"

The Tipping Point

I dump a mountain of change onto the coin machine's metal tray, press the start button, and watch in wonder as the machine eats up the quarters, dimes, and nickels I've been collecting. Counting change always feels like magic. In seconds, it's gone, like Ronan and his kibble every morning.

It's a busy evening at the Price Chopper grocery store. Shoppers pack the aisles, filling their carts with boxes of seltzer and enormous bags of chips. I'm here to cash in change so I can have a little extra spending money for my upcoming trip to New York City. I have an entire purse filled with it. I had actually been meaning to do this for years but couldn't ever find a working change machine.

My mother and I used to wrap change together into rolls of quarters and nickels at the kitchen table, then tally up the total. I loved doing that with her. What would it all amount to? It was anyone's guess.

There's always junk that doesn't belong in a change jar. At Price Chopper, I find a lot of flimsy paper clips, even the cap of a pen. A few foreign coins give me pause. They're from all the trips I took to London with Jack. I sigh and pour in another batch of coins. A ring tumbles out on top. I slam my hand against the stop button. It can't be. It is. Jack's wedding ring!

"Ma'am!" a voice calls out, a woman over at the customer service desk. She must have heard me hit the stop button. "Are you all good over there with the machine?"

My right hand is still shaking. "Yep! All good over here."

To think that all this time, Jack's wedding ring was in the change jar in our living room. We looked for the ring everywhere, and I mean everywhere, including Ronan's poop. Except, apparently, the water pitcher on the kitchen counter that became our change jar.

The logical thing to do when we realized Jack's ring was missing was to buy a new ring, but by that point I had stopped wearing my engagement ring. It didn't feel right anymore. We had two televisions on the wall in our apartment that we were watching more than each other. I moved out and dumped all the spare change into one of my old purses, knowing that Jack—a finance guy who loved Excel documents and shiny watches—would never, ever be caught rolling quarters or standing at a change machine in a grocery store like I am now. What am I supposed to do with it?

I hand my receipt to the cashier to retrieve my money in bills.

"How would you like it back?" she asks.

How would I like it back? Oh, honey, if you only knew what I got back just now. I can't concentrate on anything but Jack's ring, a simple silver band, now lassoed around my thumb, the only finger it fits on. "Twenties, I guess."

In the coming days, I catch a glimpse of the ring every time I open my wallet, alongside the wad of cash I got from the coins. It makes me think about the financial part of divorce and my yearlong alimony payments, the funny emojis Jack lists alongside every Venmo payment: a wineglass, a grilled cheese, a flamingo, a note for kale salad. Someday soon, those messages will stop, along with the payments that are helping me move along in my new life. But at least the mystery of the ring has finally been solved. I can't wait to give it back to him. Is this what it felt like when he proposed to me? I didn't see it coming, and neither will he. I decide to send him a text.

I'll be in New York tomorrow. Let's meet. I have something for you. It's killing me to not tell you what it is.

I can't think of a better place to return the ring to Jack than Vintry, our favorite bar on Stone Street at the quiet end of a pedestrian alley, one of the oldest streets in Manhattan. It was our spot, just a few blocks from our apartment. It always felt so warm and cozy, especially on winter nights when the snow floated down onto the cobblestones outside, a quiet route I walked with Ronan. I associate so many memories with that place. We had drinks there just before Hurricane Sandy hit, then after my grandmother died. Wedding anniversaries, birthdays. I even met Susan there a few times for drinks when she was in town for the Westminster Dog Show.

I had expected the bar to look the same, but everything is different when I arrive. My favorite bartenders are gone. They're playing loud dance music. The bar is filled with the white glow of cell phones. All the little candles that once illuminated whiskey bottles have vanished. It's so crowded that someone tries to snag the seat I've reserved for Jack. Every time I come to New York, I can't fathom how I ever lived here.

"All right, sweetheart?" Jack asks, tossing his coat onto the barstool.

That is one thing I love about the English: their appreciation for terms of endearment. Sweetheart, darling, love, and the like. How handsome I thought he was on our first date. We met at a dance club, then met for a drink the next night. I was about to turn thirty and on the hunt for my forever guy.

"Thank God you're here," I say. "People keep trying to steal your seat!"

He slides the wool beanie off his bald head. The tips of his ears are red. His coat smells harsh, biting, like winter.

"I ordered you a Manhattan," I say, watching him rub the palms of his hands together in delight. He's draped his wool scarf onto the back of his chair. I don't recognize it; it's not the one I bought him early on in our relationship, the one that he lost.

We sip our Manhattans, and they're as good as always. Nowhere else in the city makes them as good as Vintry. At least that hasn't changed.

"Did you hear Pulino's closed?" he asks.

I hadn't, but it always makes me sad when a restaurant I love shuts down. Jack and I spent plenty of weekends there. He looks skinnier than he was when we did that together. I doubt he's eating much pizza. That's what I brought to our relationship, a love of carbs.

He rolls up the sleeves of his shirt and takes another sip of his drink. "How's Ronan?"

"Living the dream. He's got his own yard now!"

"Can you push your chair in?" a waitress asks me.

Jack pulls out his phone. "Sorry, I need to check a work email real fast."

A dating app flashes across his screen. I look away. I don't want him to know I've seen it, but does it really matter? I guess not. I shouldn't be surprised, but I am. I had planned on giving Jack the ring at the end of the night, but I think I should do it now in case this somehow gets more awkward than it already is.

"I have something for you—close your eyes," I say, the exact thing he said when he proposed to me at a hotel in Newport, Rhode Island. We had just gotten back from dinner when I made a beeline for the bathtub. When I opened my eyes, there he was: down on one knee, also naked, holding a ring. Vintage, an old European cut, flanked by tiny diamonds on the side in the shape of angel wings. How bright the diamond was, despite how long it had been around. I remember waking up the next morning feeling like a new person. I was engaged. I belonged to someone.

Even now, after all this, I know I'll never sell my ring. I love it too much. Its meaning has changed, of course. I think more about the past when I look at it now, the person I was and how much I've changed since then. How could I ever have known what the future would bring? All we can do is say yes to the moments that feel right at the time.

I pull Jack's ring out of my wallet. Even though it's too loud in here to hear anything, I know the tiny tinkling sound the ring makes when I set it on the bar because that's what I've been doing with it all week.

I had always worried about running out of time in our relationship, but now, the minutes seem to have slowed to a crawl. No one notices that I'm staring at this ring. Even if they did, they wouldn't understand.

"Okay, ready!"

Jack opens his eyes. He recognizes his ring, but it feels as if he's seeing it again for the first time. A little chuckle slips out his mouth.

"It's your—"

"I know." He picks up the ring. "Where . . . where did you find it?"

"In the water pitcher! Our old change jar!"

He shakes his head in disbelief. "Wasn't that water pitcher a wedding present? You left it with me and made off with the wine fridge!"

I laugh. "It must have fallen off your hand when you tossed your change in there one night!"

"Fuck's sake! I can't believe it."

It truly is unbelievable. What I can't get over is that I've been dragging this purse full of change with me to every single apartment I've lived in. I thought I was leaving my divorce behind when I moved north, but all along, his ring has been with me.

"What do you want to do with it?"

Jack slides the ring onto his thumb. "I'm going to keep it, of course. I paid extra for a comfort fit!"

"Good thing I didn't sell it online, then."

"You wouldn't. Not after you stole all that change from me."

He's right. I wouldn't. I'm as attached to the ring as he is. I remember the day we picked it out, in a small boutique on the Lower East Side. We eyed the glass cases, trying on rings that we thought we'd wear for the rest of our lives. Even if that didn't come to pass, I'm so glad that I found this ring, that I could finally return it to him. Even more, that he still wants it in his life.

There is a part of me that wishes this ring could keep me in his life too. That the ring could magically fix everything, the way I hoped getting married or adopting Ronan would do, but I know now that's not how marriage works. If you don't tend to a marriage, it can easily slip away from you. That's what I will try to do differently in the future, not wait until a problem is too big to fix.

"I had always wondered what happened to it," Jack says, eyeing the ring.

Me too. No matter how many times I went over it, I couldn't figure out where the ring wound up. In hindsight, I think that what went wrong in my marriage was actually a lot like collecting change, a bunch of small things adding up over time. I don't know why I discovered the ring long after our divorce was finalized, but I still feel lucky to have found it at all.

Jack slides the ring off his thumb and places it on the bar. I don't know what he'll do with it, but that's not for me to decide. It's his ring now, not ours.

MUD SEASON

The Electra

"Can I help you?" a salesman asks. I hope so. I need retail therapy. Susan and I have come to Omer and Bob's, a local bicycle shop, in the middle of a weekday afternoon to do business. "I'm interested in that bike over there."

"Ah, the Electra."

The Electra.

I love everything about the Electra, how it feels old-timey with its thin wheels and brown leather handlebars, like the ones that Dutch women pedal over canals in Amsterdam, their knitted scarves floating in the wind. I can't think of a better time to buy it. It's mud season, and I can't seem to go anywhere in my car without getting stuck. Before I moved to New England, I had no idea what mud season was, the period between winter and spring when the dirt roads become a sloppy layer of sludge after the snow melts. If you have four-wheel drive, mud season is no big deal, but if you have a 2002 Toyota Corolla like I do, it's a lot harder to get around. I've already had to enlist a couple of strangers to push my car out of a muddy parking lot near Mount Tom.

The Electra isn't exactly suited for the hills of Vermont and New Hampshire. It seems out of place among the mountain bikes, skis, and aerodynamic bike helmets. Would an electric bike or a mountain bike be more practical?

"How would I get up a big hill?" I ask.

"You pedal," Susan replies.

Spoken like a true Capricorn. Maybe I'd ride around Dartmouth College, and some hot college professor would flag me down and ask if I wanted to discuss Shakespeare over a cheese plate. Maybe I'd lose the ten pounds I've packed on eating Susan's homecooked meals every night. Maybe I'd join a writing group and bike there and get a personal essay about my adventures with the Electra published in a magazine. All I need to make my bike vision complete is a bell and a basket on the front with a bottle of rosé.

When I lived in New York, Jack and I rented Citi Bikes around town. I still rode now and then after we divorced. I was always scared to ride on the wild streets of Manhattan, but I'd often cruise the bike path along the Hudson River in the summer, a commute much better than the smelly subway. You'd never know how sad I really was if you had seen me whizzing down the bike path in a sundress with a smile on my face. Nothing improved my mood faster than a bike ride.

Maybe Susan can get me a discount today, the way she did with the car salesmen.

"It doesn't happen to be on sale, does it?" I ask.

Susan taps her fingers on the sales counter. "It is! All Trek bikes are discounted right now."

It's strange how much this bike means to me, how captivated I am with it. Another woman is looking at it now, her fingers gripping the handlebars, like she's going to snatch it away. I absolutely don't have $500 in my checking account to blow on this bike, and it's not something I really need right now, like groceries or sex. I guess I could put it on my credit card, though I've been trying to pay off my balance, not add to it.

"It comes in other colors too," the salesman says, seeing me waver. He pulls out a catalog and flips through the pages. "We got pink . . . red . . . ivory . . ."

I point at a picture. "That one! That's the exact color of the bike I had when I was a kid."

"Seafoam."

Seafoam. Benjamin Moore couldn't have said it better himself. Light green and dreamy, the color of a Monet water lily. It's just like my first bike, a birthday present bought for me by my parents, the only bike I ever owned. I wonder where that bike is now? I rode it all the time when I was a kid, my first taste of freedom. I'd journey up my street with my friend Colleen to Katie's Korner, our local ice cream shop. I always prepared my money in advance before I left the house: a $1 bill crumbled up in a ball, plus a few quarters stuffed down inside my tight jean shorts. Sometimes I asked my mom for money. Other times, I stole it from my dad's secret stash, downstairs in the root cellar. Would he even know that $1.75 had gone missing? Even if he had, he'd probably rather let it go than confront me about it.

"Black raspberry cheesecake in a sugar cone," I said as fast as I could at the store window, so that I could spend the rest of my time breathing in the smell before she closed the window again. The smell was intoxicating. I always thought it was the ice cream that smelled so good, then I learned that the scent came from the cones, made there too.

The shop was just a mile and a half up the road, and yet it always felt so much farther. The road was busy, with no sidewalks, but the ride was always worth it when I bit into that buttery sugar cone. Maybe buying this bike will end up being another good decision.

"Done. One seafoam please."

"We don't have it in stock, so we'd have to order it for you. It'll cost extra for shipping."

Of course it will. I slide my American Express card out of my wallet and imagine an alert popping up on someone's computer in a Manhattan office, whose sole job is to monitor my credit report. *That Betsy can't control her spending one bit, can she?* And yet, I'm so happy about my decision that I don't know how I'll be able to wait two weeks until it comes in. I slip my receipt into my pocket.

"You hungry?" Susan asks.

"Always."

"Wanna get some lunch? There's a great pizza place around the corner."

Sure, I guess I can just put that on my credit card too.

As Susan and I split a large veggie pizza, I realize I am living the life of a retired person, just like Susan. I have no idea what time it is; there's nothing I should be doing at this moment. This is the exact life I wished for when I left my soulless nine-to-five job in New York: more time, freedom, the space to do something new. Now I have it, and I don't know what I'm supposed to be doing. What should my life look like? I have no clue.

What feels even more disturbing is that I feel like I'm doing something wrong by doing something different. Maeve is the only friend I have who really understands my lifestyle, what it's like to be a gig worker. From her, I've learned two important rules about how to work for yourself: It's best if you have one large, stable client, which I do—the business school at Dartmouth. I also reached out to an editor at MIT on LinkedIn and the editor of Dartmouth's alumni magazine. Now I'm writing for them too. If you want to freelance, you definitely have to hustle, but that's a trade-off I'll take to do my own thing.

And the second trick to having your own business: You need an abundance mindset, no matter what happens. You can't worry about losing money. If you *believe* you have everything you need, you *will* have everything you need. Sometimes, this feels impossible to do, especially when my paper checks get lost in the mail, but I think there's actually something to what Maeve is saying. My checks never fail to turn up after I stop obsessing over them, though that's a lot harder to do than it sounds.

While I wait for my bike to arrive from heaven, I practice an abundance mindset and head online to buy accessories. My bike will not be complete without a bell that has an ice cream cone on it, and my head will not be safe unless I have a white helmet covered in ice cream sandwiches and popsicles. I know I'm ringing up purchase after purchase, but there's a big difference between when I was a young girl stealing from her father and now. I have every intention of paying back the bank I'm borrowing from, even if it means writing freelance stories until I get carpal tunnel.

Several weeks later, my bike arrives. I'm so excited that I hop in my car the moment they call to tell me it's in.

At the shop, I hear the clicks of the bike before I even see a salesman wheel it out. I just know it's mine. "The Electra," he says, propping it up on the kickstand.

I step back to take it all in. The color is perfect; the brown leather seat is perfect. Even the reflectors on the spokes of the wheel seem to be winking at me. It's everything I imagined it would be.

"Do you want to test it out?" he asks.

I glance around the shop. There's so much I'd knock over in here: racks of bike clothing, ski boots, snowboards. "Like now?"

"Yeah, outside on the promenade."

I think of all the people out there I passed on my way in. It's been several years since I've been on a bike. How embarrassing would it be for me to fail in front of an audience? I walk the bike out the door and slide myself onto the seat. I place a foot on the left pedal and launch myself forward. I test all the gears as I pedal around pedestrians, hearing each gear click into place. I'm a little wobbly at first, but what a relief. After all this time, I still know what I'm doing.

In the coming weeks, I pedal all around Hanover, to yoga class and the gelato shop for a scoop of stracciatella. My bike is excellent at getting me out of my head. How can I feel worried about the future when I'm coasting down a hill along the Connecticut River? Even if my rear-end is sore, I always feel better when I arrive back home, like I'm just a little bit closer to getting to where I want to be, even if I'm not quite sure yet where that is.

One evening, I join Susan and Jake for a bike ride up to the Dartmouth Green. We all cycle at our own pace but never lose sight of one another. We are traveling as a unit, even if we're not riding close. This is a new experience for me, to feel like I am part of something. I have no memories of riding my bike with both of my parents.

By the time Susan, Jake, and I arrive in town, the quad is bustling with college students. We enjoy the booze and snacks Susan has packed and head back home just before sunset, the stars beginning to appear, slowly, like a magical paint-with-water coloring book.

"Hey, Betsy!" Jake yells, pedaling ahead of me. "When you get up here, you won't need to pedal again until you reach Kingsford."

It seems hard to believe, given that we're almost a mile from the house, but I loosen my grip on the brakes and coast the whole way home.

No Regrets

Something isn't right. There wasn't the usual stampede of dogs above my bedroom this morning. Susan's television isn't on, weird for a weekday morning. Crumpled tissues are strewn across the table. There's a piece of steak on the living room rug. Susan and Jake are sitting quietly in their chairs.

"What's with the steak?" I ask.

"It's a test," Susan says. "To see if Greta is dying."

Jake dabs his eyes with a tissue. I spot Greta lying on Susan's rug, her little legs splayed out behind her. At the sound of her name, her ears perk up, but she's paying no attention to the meat, unusual for Greta, the best beggar in the pack. Greta has always been excited to eat whatever I let slip from my fingertips. No matter how many times Susan has told me to not feed her dogs, I can't help myself with Greta, a retired show dog. Susan gave her the A.K.C. name No Regrets and named her after the actress Greta Garbo because of her expressive eyes.

Despite being fourteen, Greta has gotten around just fine and had plenty of energy. She barks to be let inside, then barks a few minutes later so that someone will let her out again. Her inability to make up her mind is annoying, but no one ever yells at Greta, least of all Susan, who will always be thankful to Greta for getting her through breast cancer. Of all Susan's dogs, Greta is Susan's favorite. Susan has never admitted that to me, but I've known that ever since she told me that Greta never left her side when she was off-leash.

I thought about the few times I did that with Ronan and how anxious it made me feel. The second I unclipped his leash, he ran off. Once, when we were on Cape Cod, I lost him. It was probably for only a few minutes, but that was enough time to invent plenty of nightmares: He was attacked by another dog; he drowned in the ocean; he found a new owner who carried better treats than I did. In the time he was missing, I had a flash of the life I used to have, the loneliness I experienced every day before Ronan, and a taste of what my life would become if Ronan died. I yelled Ronan's name over and over, hoping he'd return. I couldn't believe my luck when he finally did, out of breath, his long pink tongue dangling out of his mouth.

Whenever I babysat Susan's dogs, I worried Greta would die on my watch. She had Cushing's disease and always required a little more care than the others. I gave her lots of treats, hoping they would give her a reason to live one more day. As long as she stayed alive until Susan and Jake returned home, I didn't care if she peed on the carpet, barked for no reason in the middle of the night, or released farts that were so terrible I initially thought Ronan had to be behind them. They were the silent-but-violent kind, the ones that really sneak up on you.

"Come on, Ronan!" I yelled. Then I realized Ronan wasn't even in the room.

I pinched my nose. "Greta!"

She turned around and gave me a look with those brown eyes warm enough to melt a frozen New England windshield.

"Sorry, Greta. Fart all you want. You've earned it."

It isn't terribly surprising that Greta's time to cross over has arrived. She's been slowing down, and Susan and Jake have been preparing for this for a while. "I think a tumor inside her ruptured," Susan says. "We're taking her to the vet today."

"Does that mean what I think it does?"

"I don't want her to suffer anymore."

Even though I knew this would happen one day, I still don't want to hear it. Susan keeps the ashes of her departed Glens in her garage, and the thought of seeing Greta's name on a container is too much for me to handle. But will prolonging Greta's life only make it worse for her? How much suffering do you allow? How do you know when it's time? It's like walking away from a marriage. I guess at some point you just know.

"I'd like to come with you," I say.

"Are you sure?"

I don't know. I've never done this before. The only experience I have with any of this involves Galaxy, the first dog I ever had growing up in Ohio, a stray black Lab who showed up one day at our house from the wild, smelling like trash.

My mother washed him and fed him and claimed him as ours. "It's a sign!"

"Of what?" my father asked. "That other people don't take care of their dogs?"

My mother, the animal lover who was nicknamed Puss as a child because of her affection for cats, named him Galaxy. Soon, he had claimed a spot under the kitchen table.

"Absolutely not," my father said. "We already have cats!"

He tried to talk my mother out of it, but it was too late. I was already hanging on Galaxy like a jungle gym, and my mother was buying him thinly sliced bologna from the deli counter.

Years later, when I was a teenager, Galaxy developed a nagging cough that sounded so terrible I was embarrassed to have friends over. Then one day, Galaxy disappeared, the same way Ronan had vanished. Was it temporary or forever? No one knew what had happened to him until a few days later when my mother and I returned from Saturday evening Mass. My father left a Post-it note inside on the countertop. Usually, it was my mother who penned notes in her romantic script, telling me of the phone calls I had missed from a friend or crush. My father's handwriting was barely legible, in slanted capital letters. It always seemed as jarring as our relationship, something I couldn't ever make sense of. He was heading out to work the midnight shift and wanted us to know that he had found Galaxy.

He was down by the brook, where I knew he'd be.

My first experience with death, and I was reading about it on a Post-it note. How could a piece of paper so small contain such enormity?

My dad's note isn't unlike the tiny piece of steak that Susan picks up off the floor and places on the counter. She washes her hands and stares out the window, birds flying to and from the feeder. "We should get going."

"Let me just run and get my purse. I'll buy you a coffee after the appointment. Or something stronger. Whatever you want."

"Are you sure you want to come along for this? Do you think you'll be able to handle it?"

I will swallow my tears if I need to. Greta isn't my dog, but I love her all the same. "I'd like to be there for you."

Susan hands Jake another tissue, then heads out to start the car. I hold the front door for Jake, who's carrying Greta in a fuzzy yellow blanket. We sit in the car, waiting. Susan hesitates. The windshield wipers squeak back and forth. I don't know how I'll ever do this with Ronan, but I know one day, I'll have to let go. How strange that we're somehow able to love so willingly, even when we know that one day, everything will end.

Even my father, the stoic who had been so against Galaxy years ago, couldn't let go. He went out searching for him. My father knew where to look, back to the wild, to a spot in the woods that was beloved by all of us, where we went creek-walking in the summertime. My father dug a hole with his shovel and buried Galaxy right there where he took his last breath.

Now, it's Greta's time to say good-bye. Jake is in the back seat of Susan's car holding her; she's adorable as always, wrapped up like a burrito, with her heart-shaped head and two pointy ears sticking out the edge of the blanket. Susan glances at Jake in the rearview mirror, then shifts the car into drive. None of us are ready to let go, except for Greta. Her eyes say it all.

Take-Out Terror

I enter 911 on my cell phone and hover my finger on the keypad, ready to dial if I need to. For the last hour, Ronan has been barking nonstop by the back door. He rarely barks in the middle of the night. He loves sleep as much as I do. Something isn't right.

I'm too scared to leave my bed, and I can't even sneak upstairs and wake Susan and Jake to tell them I'm about to be murdered because they're out of town. Am I allowed to call 911 to tell them I *think* someone is out there?

I thought I had it made earlier when Susan and Jake took off in their RV with their dogs for several weeks. I had the entire house all to myself. I couldn't wait! No more yelling, no early morning running of the dogs, no recycling lectures from Jake. No one tossing stale water from the dog bowls over the side of the deck. For once, I could sleep in past six in the morning.

After Susan and Jake pulled out of the driveway (with Susan driving, of course), I fled upstairs to their deck with Ronan in tow. I got cushions out for both of us and plopped onto a chair next to him and thought: *How wonderful life would be if I were a homeowner like Susan and Jake, people who own more than three dinner plates!*

And then—my phone rang. It was Susan. Typical. Already calling to check in.

"Do you miss us?"

I had just opened a bottle of rosé, popped a frozen pizza in the oven, and taken off my pants. "Hell no!" I said, a lone squirrel the only paparazzi in sight.

"You're not snooping around our house, are you?"

"I did that ages ago. And you told me that I could use your deck when you were away."

"That's fine. But water the plants for me while you're up there, will you?"

I turned on the hose and gave them a good soak, staying until dusk, then rounded up Ronan so we could start getting ready for bed. I shut Susan's patio door, but the door wouldn't lock. I called Susan.

"Do you miss us yet?" she asked.

"Did you know—"

"Jake, watch where you're going!"

"Listen to me!" I yell.

"It's getting dark, and we need to pull off. Say a prayer to help us find a Walmart parking lot before my husband wrecks the RV."

"Did you know that the door to your deck doesn't lock?"

"We never lock our doors. Why do you care? Are you throwing a party and trashing our house?"

"I don't have enough friends to do that. Maeve is my only friend, and she's with her boyfriend this weekend. But more importantly, what do you mean, 'We never lock our doors'?"

"Who's going to come into my house? We have four dogs. If anyone can get past them, then they can have whatever the fuck they want."

Who doesn't lock their doors? In New York City, my apartments had several locks, including a deadbolt, but with so many people around, I rarely worried about my safety. My doormen monitored who came and went but looked the other way when I walked in late at night with a date. Laughter from my neighbors seeped through the walls. Delivery guys rapped on doors with pizza deliveries. In eleven years, I never worried about anyone robbing me or breaking into my apartment.

The one place I was scared to be alone was in my own home after my mother's death. It was so quiet without her. Every noise seemed magnified, the furnace or water pump kicking on, the soft creak of a floorboard. It didn't matter that I was a young adult. If my father wasn't home, I'd sleep with all the lights on.

Now in Susan's house, it feels like that all over again, with no one to save me but Ronan. I have one dog, not four like Susan does. Could Ronan kill someone for me if he needed to? All I can do is hope that if someone wants to rob me, they will take what they need from upstairs and leave me alone, the girl living in the basement with not much to her name. Hopefully, whoever is out there sees my beat-up car and decides they're better off robbing the Dartmouth kids with the Jeep Wranglers.

I flip a light on, then turn it off. Each hour that passes, the moon slithers farther west through the pine trees. I've always loved the sight of it from my backyard, but you couldn't pay me enough to go out there for a better view of it right now. Ronan's still focused on the back door. Is the murderer hiding in Jake's shed? The only time Ronan takes his eyes off the door is to make sure I am still awake. If only he had been this fearless in New York City when I had a mouse problem. He's made quite the transformation since we've come back to Hanover. Absolutely fearless.

Meanwhile, all I can think about is the opening scene in the movie *Scream* with Drew Barrymore, a telephone ringing in an isolated house in the middle of nowhere, the star actress getting killed off in the first ten minutes of the film. I imagine Susan's landline ringing upstairs, the one that always announces Bernie Sanders' campaign people, but this time, it will reveal the identity of the man who plans to kill me. What do I have to defend myself? I have butter knives. I have matches. Could I do damage with a Swiffer?

My eyelids feel so heavy. A rustling in the brush jolts me back awake. Did I actually hear the noise, or was I dreaming it? How long was I asleep? Ten minutes? I can't spend my entire night like this. I open my medicine cabinet and pop a couple of NyQuil just like old times. I guess at least if I go tonight, I won't have to worry about paying my credit card bills. My father will probably go to Massachusetts to pick up my remains instead of New Hampshire. What about Ronan? Who will take him? I don't have a will. I don't want Susan to rehome him with some rich couple on Martha's Vineyard.

I remember the story she told me once, about a murder that happened down the street, long before I got here, when two Dartmouth College professors were stabbed to death by a couple of teenagers. She mentioned it one night when we were all hanging out in her living room. It sounded so outrageous that I didn't believe her, but then I Googled it—she wasn't lying. It was all over the Internet, proof that bad things can happen anywhere.

I close my eyes again. Hours later, the faint chirping of birds rustles me awake. I find the latest issue of the *New Yorker* on my chest. I've never been more grateful to see a hint of daylight. Ronan is passed out at the bottom of the bed. What a night. I pick up my phone and dial Susan. I can't imagine spending another night here alone.

"Where are you? You've gotta come back home!"

"Jake! Pay attention to the road! I should've never let him drive today."

I miss being part of their banter. Maybe I should have convinced them to take me with them. "How long would it take you to drive back?"

"Forever. We just crossed into Virginia. Why?"

"I think someone tried to break into the house."

"Why would they need to break in when you did them a favor and left the door unlocked? If you had taken CBD like I told you to, you'd sleep right through someone killing you. Why aren't you taking it yet? It will change your life."

It annoys me that Susan isn't worried about this. Why isn't she taking this seriously? "I mean it! I was really scared."

"Betsy..."

Oh God, another lecture.

"This is life in the country. We got coyotes, deer, fisher cats, all sorts of things with four legs that come out in the night. No one is going to come in and kill you. There aren't enough people in town to do that."

I'm not the least bit reassured. What if my perpetrator comes back? Maybe I could pull a chair in front of the door. Or sneak into Susan and Jake's alcohol stash and have a whiskey before I go to bed? I wish Susan were here to make me a Manhattan.

I venture upstairs and check all the doors. No evidence that anyone was inside. No mud on the hardwood floor, all the family photographs and colorful paintings still horizontal. No dirty martini glasses in the sink, no butter-smudged fingerprints on the fridge. Susan and Jake's favorite *Jeopardy!* chairs are empty. Haven't even thought about watching the show without them here. What's the point in playing alone?

I head to the backyard to investigate. I haven't really ever missed New York since I left, not even when my *New York Times* or *New Yorker* magazine arrived in the mail and advertised a new Italian restaurant or cocktail bar. But now, as I wander around the backyard looking for clues and footprints as if I'm on *Law & Order*, I wish I were standing on a crowded subway platform, surrounded by hundreds of miserable people.

A trail of trash by Jake's shed catches Ronan's attention. He rushes off to investigate, his tail wagging high. "Good boy, Ronan!" I follow him over to inspect the scene. It appears as if someone or something has knocked the garbage bin to the ground. The lid is a good distance away, on the hillside down by the brook. I can't believe how much garbage is on the ground. I must have left the lid loose on the garbage bin when I took it out yesterday. Jake would really give me hell for that one. Home isn't home unless he's here trying to get me to clean up my act.

I paw through each piece of trash, dropping bug-covered food into bags. Week-old, soggy coffee grounds and moldy carrots stir up an unexpected nostalgia. They remind me of all my walks with Ronan in the city, where the streets in the Financial District were lined with so many rows of trash bags that pedestrians had to walk around them single file.

The difference between then and now is that there are giant claw marks on the plastic container that once held my Thai food from a few nights ago. Sharp nails, far too big to belong to a raccoon, have sliced right through spongy plastic that didn't stand a chance. I may be a city girl who jumps at the sound of a squirrel running through the brush, but I've been here long enough to know a thing or two. Those are bear claws. Susan's never going to believe this! I dial her number.

"Again so soon? Do you miss me?" she asks.

I do. What a difference twelve hours makes.

TOMATO SEASON

Adventures in Tubing

I step inside the small general store, while Annie and Bridget linger behind. We wander down an aisle with dusty floors, the shelves filled with Vermont maple syrup, eggs from a farm down the road, and stacks of firewood from last season.

"Are we in the wrong place?" Annie asks, a straw hat in hand. Her legs are pale from spending the summer in an air-conditioned office.

I've asked myself this question plenty of times since I've been in New England, like the time I walked a half mile uphill to reach an unmarked swimming hole. "I don't think so. Yelp said this is the Midway Station."

"But I don't see any inner tubes," Bridget says.

Strange. Someone mentioned that this is supposed to be the perfect spot to rent inner tubes to float down the White River.

Bridget and Annie have been visiting for only a few days, and I feel desperate to show them a good time. So far, we've had cocktails at Pine and gone to a brewery. Is there more to New England than eating and drinking, or is it just what I do best? I've taken them around to the coffee shops where I do my writing, and when they complain about their jobs, I feel grateful that I'm here doing my own thing, even if some days I worry about my checks not arriving on time.

I had suggested tubing when they arrived from New York City, wanting to give them the real New England experience, or at least what I thought was the real New England experience. In New York, we sat on bar stools and on park benches sipping $5 lattes. When I left the city last year, I worried that we might lose touch with each other. Would the Moon Squad—our exclusive little astrological club—survive if we weren't in the same city?

I spot a man who has a wandering eye that I hope wasn't caused by a tubing accident. "Is this the place with the inner tubes?" He points to the back wall, where a half dozen enormous inner tubes are propped up on top of each other. How did we miss that?

Bridget and Annie have something to say about everything, but they're unusually quiet right now. None of us have ever been tubing before, but it seems like it would be relaxing.

Once I see the inner tubes, I realize this isn't going to work. There's no way they're going to fit in my car. I should have thought this through more.

"Is that your pickup outside?" I ask the man behind the counter, interrupting the conversation he's just been having about a cow gone missing. "The white truck outside in the parking lot?" I ask. It has to be. It's the only one out there. "Could you drive us up the river? We'll pay you."

He hesitates. Was it wrong of me to ask?

"I get off in twenty minutes. If you can wait, I'll take you a mile up the road, then you can just float back but put some sunscreen on. You're gonna fry out there today."

Of all the weekends Annie and Bridget could come, this was probably the worst one. It's hotter here than in New York City. The house doesn't have air conditioning, but I bought floor fans before they got here. A dip in the river will feel amazing if we can somehow make it there. "We can wait."

"Okay, but I have to warn you, the back of my truck is a little dirty."

I pull a twenty out of my wallet for the inner tubes. "We don't mind!"

We wheel our inner tubes into the parking lot and slip into the shade. Bridget slathers on sunscreen, then slips off her sneakers. "Won't be needing these!" This is what I've always loved about Bridget, that she's up for anything.

Annie takes a photo of the truck's license plate. "I'm sending this to my brother. Just in case."

"In case of what?" I ask.

"If we go missing."

"It's going to be fine!"

"I don't know. Are we sure this is a good idea?"

"Listen, if we survived that hellhole agency job full of male chauvinists, can't we handle a relaxing afternoon floating down the river in inner tubes? If you wanna back out now, this is your chance."

Bridget dons sunglasses. "I'm in." She brushes her bangs out of her eyes and climbs into the man's truck wearing her halter top bathing suit.

Annie puts on her straw hat. "Someone's got to supervise both of you."

The man leans out his window. "Maybe one of you should get in the back with the tubes so they don't fly out?"

I've had a good life and not much to lose, no boyfriend who will miss me, no full-time job where my coworkers would have to take on my assignments after attending my funeral. "I'll go."

Wearing a strapless purple two piece, I jump into the truck bed, then realize that when the driver said the back of his truck was a little dirty, he meant full of actual dirt. I wrap my arms around all three inner tubes as if they are giant plush teddy bears, and as we cruise down the winding road, I try to come up with legitimate reasons he might need a truck full of dirt, wholesome Vermont hobbies like composting and gardening projects, and not for burying our bodies down by the river. If he's going to murder anyone, it'll be me, since I'm already dirty now.

I wonder what they're all talking about inside the truck. Bridget would probably just ask him outright in Scorpio fashion, "You're not going to kill us, are you?" whereas Annie wouldn't say a word because she'd be secretly taking screenshots of her location and sending them to the police.

The driver pulls off to the side of the road, takes the $10 I've given him for his time, then waves goodbye to us as we stand in our bathing suits holding the inner tubes.

"Now what?" Annie asks.

"Fuck, it's hot out here," Bridget says.

Rule number one of tubing—there is apparently a good time to float, and I haven't picked it, not in the middle of a summertime drought when the river is shallow. From high up on the road, the river seemed full, but now as we stand at the river's edge, I see that's not the case. I had imagined all three of us coasting down the river, under covered bridges, past rolling farmland, twisting around wooded hillsides, not skidding along rocks jutting out from the water like icebergs.

Bridget sniffs her inner tube. "I wonder if my tube is burning. It kind of smells like hot rubber."

"Should we turn around?" Annie asks, the cautious project manager weighing the odds, always thinking of what could go wrong. It seems funny now to think how supportive she was when I wanted to quit my job. Maybe she realized that me staying in New York was a far worse option than moving to New England. But does she have a point? Should we give up? Maybe I'd still be at that job if she hadn't given me a push. Maybe she needs the same from me right now, a little encouragement.

Bridget splashes her tube down into the water. "I'm barefoot. There's only one way back, and that's this godforsaken river. Let's go." Braver than the rest of us, like always. It reminds me of the time she gave a client presentation while breaking up with her boyfriend on G-chat.

Annie and I toss our inner tubes into the river, then wiggle our butts into the holes as we prepare to get the weirdest tan lines we've ever had. Within seconds, my flip-flops slide off my feet. I thrust my arm into the water to catch them.

"Wait up!" I yell to Annie and Bridget.

I try to paddle my way down the river to catch them, but a current sweeps my inner tube in the wrong direction and traps me behind a triangular rock. This feels just like life. You float along for a while, then before you know it, you're stuck.

I position my legs against the rock, give a hearty push, and drift back down the river toward them. How long have I been waiting for today, a lazy afternoon with my friends, and then this—a trail of blood floating behind me. I must have cut myself somewhere on one of the rocks.

"Jesus! That one really hurt!" Annie yells.

I paddle so hard to reach them that my bathing suit bottom inches up into my butt crack. I reach them just before the highway overpass. Bridget leans an arm out to catch me. "Jesus, look at that. Sunburned already, in Vermont of all places. I have my Irish heritage to thank for that."

I know I'll be covered in bruises later and that Bridget and Annie will probably ream me out for this, but the strange thing is that I'm actually having a good time. I know that this is something we'll talk about for the rest of our lives—*Hey, Bets, remember that one time you took us tubing and nearly killed us?* Trying to navigate this crazy world together feels just like old times, except instead of trying to get through terrible client meetings in New York, we're trying to get out of this river without needing stitches. It makes me think of what Annie asked earlier—*Are we in the right place?* I never thought I'd say this, but I actually think I am.

Does this make me an official New Englander? I remember the time I drove past a *Road Closed* sign. Someone had added *REALLY* above the sign because so many people had ignored the sign and drove down the road anyway. There's a "Yes, you can!" spirit New Englanders have that I never thought I'd learn to embrace, the type of gumption that propels locals to drive down roads that are clearly marked off-limits. Well, here I am, the new New England me, tubing down a nearly empty river trying to make it work.

I know I'll think of Annie and Bridget every time I drive past this spot, even when the river is frozen six months from now. Who knows where my life will be then, but I think for now, it's time to get my friends back on land.

"Should we call it a day and just go to a bar?" I ask. "My ass and legs are bruised, and I have a terrible wedgie."

Bridget sighs with relief, grasping her inner tube. "I thought you'd never ask."

Small House for an Artist's Family

Today's a big day at Susan's house. A few weeks ago, we found out that an architecture critic would be coming to the house to write a story about the Hunter architects who designed our house in 1957. Susan has been preparing ever since. There isn't a spot of dog hair on the rug. Piles of magazines and newspapers are stacked by date on the coffee table. Someone, presumably Jake, even scraped a longtime mosquito carcass off the wall.

The dogs are all out on the deck, balancing on their hind legs, rattling the screen door to get in. "Stop it all of you!" Susan yells, leaning on the counter. "That's all I need. A hole in the screen door before she gets here. How would I explain that?"

"Hmmm. You could tell her it makes your house more original," I say.

Susan has even gone to the trouble of placing old newspaper clippings about the house on the counter. One article calls our home a "Small House for an Artist's Family" because the original owner ran the art department at Dartmouth College and hung his own paintings on the wood-paneled walls.

Susan told me once that her house was often chosen when someone wanted a tour of a Hunter home. I thought of the chipped paint peeling off the home's exterior like the rind of a lemon. "Because you haven't fixed it up?"

"Because it's the most original!" she snapped back.

So, now here we are, doing our best to spruce up a sixty-year-old home. Susan is sweating profusely, trying to erase an old water stain on the breakfast bar that's one of my favorite features of the house and a recent addition. Susan had a carpenter build it using wood that her father had from walnut trees at their childhood home. Given that Susan and I are both from Ohio, it feels special when I sit at the counter, as if I'm summoning our ancestral heritage to solve my problems.

"What is that?" Susan says, eyeing the rosé wine bottle in my hands. The label on the bottle is shaped like the state of New Hampshire. "It's called 'Live Free Rosé!' Isn't that creative? Like, 'Live free or die' but the wine version."

Susan wipes a dust bunny off the side of her black leggings. "I thought you were getting Miraval. I told you to get that brand. You were the one who told me that it's from Brad Pitt and Angelina Jolie's winery in France."

"They're divorced now."

"So you have that in common."

"I know, but the co-op didn't have Miraval."

"I want her to have Miraval, only the best."

"Maybe the New Hampshire liquor outlet has it? I'll go look."

"No. I'll use it as an excuse to send Jake on an errand. He's annoying me." Susan leans over to turn on the vacuum, then stops to catch her breath.

"Are you having an asthma attack? Do you need your inhaler? Please don't die."

"I think I might. I have so much more to do."

It doesn't look that way. Everything is neat and tidy, though I have to admit that something seems off. Then it hits me. "Where's the television?"

"I took it down."

"Why? Do you think you're taking this a little too far?"

"A flat screen isn't appropriate to the time period. I want her to have an authentic experience. I know how to stage a room."

"Who cares about the television? Tell her you smoke up every night and watch Rachel Maddow. She'll love that."

Jake appears at the screen door, sweaty and weary. Susan must have had him cleaning the deck and scooping up all the dog poops. "Oh, hi,

Betsy," he says, his voice soft.

"Jake, you don't have time to socialize with Betsy! I need you to go to the store and get Miraval."

Jake scratches his head. "What's Miraval?"

"Do you want me to go get it?" I ask.

"No! You need to tell me what else is missing."

I scan the room. "Jake's chair." I thought the room looked kind of empty. "Why'd you move it?"

"Not original to the time period."

"You don't want me in some kind of midcentury-modern costume, do you?" Maybe I should just make myself scarce.

"How about one of your nice dresses?"

"Are you kidding me? There's no way my New York dresses fit anymore. Can't I just wear spandex?"

"No, and she'll probably want to see your apartment, so make sure to clean your bedroom and put your vibrator away."

I spin around and head downstairs. If the architecture critic lives in Brooklyn, she's probably been to Babeland too, but I do like I'm told and detach my vibrator from its charger, toss it into the top drawer of my dresser, then head straight for the bathroom with cleaning supplies. Unfortunately, my tub has somehow managed to attract a bug, one so big that he actually had the muscle to push up through the plug. Taking the shower wand, I aim directly at the bug's enormous wings and flush the beast on his merry way down the drain, outside, and into whatever river he can go tubing in like every other Dartmouth College student on the Connecticut River.

"Oh, did you used to live in Brooklyn?" I imagine The Critic asking, upon seeing my astrology books and tortoise-shell glasses on the coffee table. As I wipe Pledge on my desk with a rag, I imagine how the evening will unfold. We will sit on my couch and laugh as Ronan licks summer sweat off her legs, his way of welcoming her into the house. She will then return to Brooklyn and introduce me to her editor at *The New Yorker*, where I will embark on a new career of writing cartoon captions and freelance stories on where to find the best breakfast sandwich in New England.

By midafternoon I've showered and dressed myself just in time for The Critic's arrival. I was hoping maybe I'd get a chance to pre-game, but she's arrived a little early.

I can only be grateful that I haven't yelled out, "I feel like a whale in this dress!" on my way back upstairs because The Critic is standing on the top step wearing a T-shirt, shorts, and shiny gold Birkenstocks. Weird. Who wears gold Birkenstocks? A New Yorker visiting the country? Even I didn't do that when I came to pick up Ronan, though he might be interested in those as a chew toy. Other than that, she looks like all the photos I saw of her online when Susan and I did a little stalking: rectangular spectacles, hair swept back off her face.

Jake is splashed out in a polo shirt, and Susan is the most glamorous I've ever seen her, in bright red lipstick and a sleeveless black cotton dress. I've arrived in a floral spaghetti-strap dress with a poofy skirt.

"Welcome to my home," Susan says. "This is Jake, my husband."

"And I'm Betsy."

"Are you their daughter?" The Critic asks.

"No, no. I'm their tenant, and I live downstairs in the—" Susan shoots me a look that says, *Don't screw this up for me.* "In the *garden* apartment."

Susan wastes no time delving into the story of how the house came into their possession. I realize I have never heard her tell it before. Strangely, it all happened the same summer I got married in England. Eight bidders emerged the day the house went on the market, but Susan and Jake were the lucky buyers.

"We had to do a lot of work when we moved in," Susan explains, pointing to wooden slats holding up the countertop. "The entire kitchen was painted peach. Peach! Why would you do that?"

I've been living here for nearly a year and thought I knew everything, but now I wonder how many other secrets of the house have slipped past me. I peer down into the cracks behind the fridge, and sure enough, there are traces of pale peach paint.

Another mystery that needs some explaining—why isn't The Critic smiling? She's walking around nodding her head, but doesn't seem very impressed. Maybe she has a bad case of resting bitch face? I know I did in New York.

"One of my favorite things about the living room is this enormous window!" I say, as if I'm pulling back an imaginary curtain with my hands. "It's wonderful when the snow falls."

"Every window evokes a different mood," The Critic says.

She's right about that. My bedroom window is nestled down in a hollow, perfect for crying in secret. I never need to go to the Nugget, the only movie theater in town, when my bedroom window puts on a spectacular show, especially during a rainstorm. I've seen a frog jump up and down against the window, trying to get in, and a tiny lizard glue himself to the window, giving me an R-rated view of his underbelly. In the span of a day, I once watched a spider catch a moth, descend down onto it, and finish it off slowly like a seven-course tasting meal.

"If you'll follow me over here, this staircase leads to the *garden* apartment," Susan says.

I remember how enamored I was the first time I saw the wooden staircase. The Critic tilts her head up toward the circular skylight, then snaps a photo with her iPhone. I flip on a light switch, the way I do in the winter when I stumble back downstairs after one of Susan's cocktails. One night, I had too many drinks, missed a step, and fell on my rear end.

The Critic points to the tear-shaped light fixtures dangling from the ceiling.

"All original," Susan says.

We amble down the circular staircase, skipping right past the small laundry room with the washer and dryer that have Jake's labels on them. I scooch ahead of both of them, preparing to open the door to show The Critic the best feature of the house: Ronan. He hasn't made a sound, but I know he's on the other side ready to pounce. I twist the doorknob. Ronan lunges through the open door. The Critic spins around to avoid him. Oh, no ... she doesn't like dogs.

I coax Ronan toward me, then shoo him outside. His ears drop when he realizes he's being left alone in an empty yard. *What the*—? his expression says.

"She doesn't like dogs," I whisper, patting his furry bum. He licks my face. I rub the inside of his ears, his favorite spot, and he groans a little.

"Don't worry, baby. Mommy doesn't like her either. But you need to stay in the backyard until she leaves . . ."

I rejoin Susan and The Critic upstairs, where Susan's deck has been transformed into a Williams-Sonoma ad. All four chairs actually have their cushions on them for once, arranged around the table. Her potted plants have grown so lush that it's hard to tell where one stops and the next begins. I touch one of the cushions to see if it's damp, but this isn't an ordinary day, where someone's forgotten to put them under the awning during a rainstorm. Even the garden hose is out of sight.

"Would you like something to drink?" Susan asks.

"No, I'm fine," The Critic replies.

"We have rosé! Miraval. From Angelina Jolie's winery in France."

She shakes her head. "Do you mind if I walk around the back of the house?"

Jake escorts her down the wooden steps, through Susan's garden, past the clothesline, and up the hill.

"She'll be covered in ticks," Susan whispers.

"Her funeral."

We complete the tour back inside in the living room, where Susan demonstrates her favorite part about the house: a swing door on the white stucco fireplace. "Only a good architect would design it like this."

The Critic snaps a few more pictures. "What's it like here in the winter?"

A bar. A dark one that smells like weed and whiskey.

"Cozy," I reply.

Susan hands The Critic her business card, with contact information and a photo of her Glens. "Call me if you have any questions."

She nods, then walks out with Jake. The door opens, then slams shut. Jake returns and heaves a sigh. "She's gone."

"This dress makes me feel fat!" I say. "I can't wait to take it off."

"Before you get naked, help me take off the expensive Marimekko tablecloth first. I don't want Jake to spill any shit on it."

Within minutes, Susan's dogs rush out. Ronan's still in the backyard, barking.

"Jake, open the wine and grab the wineglasses!" Susan yells.

I kick off my sandals and take a seat. "Do you regret going through all the trouble now after meeting her? Cleaning and rearranging everything?"

"Absolutely not. I wanted her to love my home the way I do. Don't you love it here?"

I do. I love Susan's house so much that sometimes I fantasize about coming into money so that I can buy it from her and make it mine if Susan and Jake ever decide to move. I'd put a writing desk in what used to be the artist's studio, where the first owner did all his painting, right in front of the big window that overlooks the ravine. I'd also install an outdoor shower so that I could bathe naked with the white pines. I can't fathom the thought of anyone else living here but me. Even if my name isn't on the mortgage, this feels like my house too.

"Can we talk about her gold Birkenstocks?" Susan asks. "How fucking weird was that?"

"Really weird." I prop my bare feet up on a cushion. "Maybe it's a Brooklyn thing."

The Critic's article comes out a few weeks later. She's far more effusive on the page than in person. She pays homage to my favorite part of the house—the circular staircase—and highlights something else I didn't know. When the house was first constructed, part of the exterior was painted yellow and blue.

I keep thinking about what moving day must have been like for Susan and Jake, trying to manage five dogs while, on the other side of the Atlantic, I walked down the aisle with Jack, thinking we would be together for a lifetime. Maybe in some twisted New England backroad kind of way, my future was aligning with Susan's, landing us here at this very moment, without us even knowing.

Driving Miss Daisy

"My parents can't believe you're driving me around to help me ace my driving test!" Daisy yells from the passenger seat of my car.

We're cruising along a deserted highway, but I can barely hear her. We have all the windows down because my air conditioning isn't working. I don't know if it was ever working.

When I'm not out covering small-town stories for the newspaper, I'm with Daisy.

She's sixteen, full of optimism, and a breath away from earning her license. Daisy's family owns Ronan's sister Lilli, so Daisy feels like my family too. We usually meet up when she gets out of school in the afternoon. Susan thinks it's odd that I'm hanging out with a teenager. So does Daisy's mother. The only ones who don't think it's weird are Daisy and me.

"I really appreciate your help!" she yells.

Oh, to be young again, like Daisy, with dewy, wrinkle-free skin, thick eyebrows, and chocolate-brown hair, free of tiny gray strands like mine. "Just tell your dad to return the favor and set me up with that friend of his! What's his name again? Fergus?"

Daisy's laugh rattles in her chest. I love that sound, not a trace of sadness to be found. "Angus!"

We're out driving today to get some more practice because she failed her driver's test. I did the same thing when I was a kid, even though I was extra cautious. When my test was over, I pulled back into the parking lot of the Department of Motor Vehicles and waited. My instructor was writing a lot. I assumed he was making notes about my performance for future students to follow. Then he told me I failed. My turns were too wide. If only he could see them now.

I pull off the highway exit and pop a piece of gum in my mouth. "So, what happened exactly?"

"I ran a red light."

That's way worse than wide turns. "You ran a red light during your test?"

"I think it was invisible. It came out of nowhere."

I've never heard of an invisible red light. "How many points off is that?"

"It's an automatic fail. That's why I want to take you to where I did my test, to practice more."

I have to admit that I'm curious about this invisible stoplight, if my eyesight is still good enough to spot it.

Daisy reminds me a lot of myself in high school but the much cooler version. Like I was, she's a theater nerd but better because she got the lead role of Ariel in *The Little Mermaid*. She's really into boys, also like me, but better because she gets dates with guys who woo her with pizza and candles. Yes, she's a teenager, but half the time, she's the one parenting me, telling me I should sleep over because her mom and I had too much wine with dinner.

She's so responsible that I forget there's a twenty-one-year age difference between us. The first time it hit me was the night of the winter play at Hanover High School. Daisy and I went together. I stood by the lockers, minding my own business, scouting the lobby for single dads while Daisy picked up our tickets. I couldn't remember the last time I set foot in a high school, a world so foreign to me now.

A student in glasses approached me as I was counting wedding rings on men's fingers.

"Excuse me," she said.

I moved to the side so she could get into her locker.

"Are you Daisy's mom?"

Was it finally time for Botox? No one had ever asked me that in my entire life, mistaken me for a mom. "Me?"

The girl nodded.

"No. I'm not her mother. I'm her friend." *Her much older friend.* I did the math in my head, tapped out the years on my fingers. It was possible for me to be Daisy's mom, but I would've had to have given birth to Daisy when I was twenty-one, and having children would've been the last thing on my mind then because my mother had just died. Her comment did give me pause—why had I gone to the play? Surely, I could have gone to a bar or done something else people my age do. Part of me must have been curious about what this would be like, to go to a high school play with a teenage girl who was young enough to be my daughter. Was I subconsciously auditioning for motherhood?

"Do I look old enough to be your mom?" I asked Daisy when she returned with our tickets. "That's what your friend said. Well, she didn't say that exactly, but it was implied . . ."

Daisy swept her long brown hair up into a ponytail with a rubber band from her wrist, then laughed. "Absolutely not, you look like you're in your twenties."

"God, I love you."

"I love you too." Daisy cracked open her can of Coke. "You're not old. She's just weird. Don't worry about it."

We wandered into the auditorium and found our seats. Surrounded by teenagers texting in crop tops, I'd been foolish to think there might be single dads around. I was a single thirty-seven-year-old woman at a high school play. If anyone was weird, it was clearly me.

After the show, Daisy spent the night. The next morning, I dropped her off at school, not with a lunch of organic hard-boiled eggs and a garden-fresh mesclun salad like the other moms, but with Diet Coke and Cheetos. I know Daisy likes Cheetos because we feed them to her dog Lilli. I keep a respectable distance away from the school so I won't embarrass Daisy with my old car, although she doesn't seem to mind. She always seems genuinely happy to see me.

Driving Daisy gives me a sense of purpose. I like feeling needed. Sometimes Daisy's friend Sydney joins, who's also in the process of getting her license. They talk about boys a lot.

"Girls," I say, lowering the music. "I don't want to tell you this, but you're going to be complaining about boys for the rest of your lives."

When Daisy gripes about school and her homework, I try to put her problems in perspective. "Listen, now that we have the iPhone to do everything for us, you'll never need any of the stuff you're studying for, especially math."

"My mom majored in math."

"Oh. Well, don't tell your mom I said that then."

Daisy offers dating advice so wise it could appear on tank tops. When I ask her if I should proposition a man I keep seeing around on Dartmouth's campus, she says that if I don't, I might be waiting a while.

"The only guys who are bold are gay," she says.

I never expected that my life in New England would involve hanging out with teenagers, but it makes sense. My day-to-day existence feels a lot like it did when I was in high school. I don't have a full-time job. Boyfriends and money are elusive. I shave my legs every several weeks. Every day feels like it did when I was a teenager, an uphill climb, more confusing than the one that has come before, but hanging out with Daisy makes life feel more manageable.

When we arrive in town, the scene of her driver's test, we find a parking lot and switch places in the car. As soon as I plop down into the passenger seat, I realize I've done something really stupid. I forgot my car registration and insurance information at home. It's all still in a folder from when I applied for my New Hampshire driver's license. I'm not wearing a low-cut top either, which will make talking myself out of a ticket even more difficult. What kind of example am I setting for the future generation?

"Listen, Daisy," I say. She's already got both hands on the wheel, ready to do business. "I know we're only supposed to be practicing, but I need you to drive really well because if we get pulled over, you might have to pick me up from prison. I left all my paperwork at home."

She shifts the car in reverse. "No problem," she says, before I have a chance to second-guess myself. "I just want to find the invisible traffic light, and then we're out of here."

Daisy pulls out onto the road. I glance in my side-view mirror at the sour expression on the driver behind us. Are we driving too slow? He tries to pass us, then swerves back into his lane.

"You can go a little faster," I say. "Just don't do that when you take the actual test."

Daisy glances at the speedometer. "I'm going the speed limit."

Maybe it's broken, like the air conditioning. I tell myself to stop micromanaging her, but when she pulls over to the side of the road, I have to intervene. "Why are you stopping?"

"Hill start."

What in the hell is a hill start? Apparently, demonstrating how to start your car on an incline is required in Vermont. How did I make it through the New England winter not knowing how to do this? She shifts into park, then yanks on the emergency brake.

My eyes dart around, looking for police cars, as Daisy narrates her every move slowly, as if reading a children's book. "And here's where my instructor made me parallel park . . . this is where I turned . . . how am I doing?"

She's actually doing great. She waits a good three seconds at stop signs and doesn't totally pause, like Alicia Silverstone did in *Clueless*, one of my favorite movies from the nineties when I learned how to drive. She doesn't inch forward under a stoplight and mutter the f-word like I do, thinking this will somehow cause the light to turn faster. Daisy is going to pass her test, hands down. What will happen then? Will she still have time for me? Is this what all mothers worry about?

We round a bend in the direction of the elusive red light. While it isn't invisible, it is a little deceiving. It's low to the ground and hidden off to the side. Those DMV jerks! Trying to trick young, aspiring drivers.

"I see what you mean," I say. "But now you know it's there. Just don't run it next time, and you'll be fine."

We return the car to where we started and switch places. Time for a little speeding. I've never been more excited to be behind the wheel again.

"Did I do a good job?" she asks.

"Absolutely. Don't worry. You're going to nail it."

More than once today I thought of something Annie told me after I froze my eggs and got only four, when it seemed that maybe motherhood wasn't in my future: *There's lots of ways to be a mom*. Maybe mothering someone like Daisy will be enough to fill that void if I don't have children of my own. I hope so.

While I still have her, we stop off for pizza and ice cream, then head back into town so that I can drop her off at school for her evening choir concert. I don't know why I like pulling into the Hanover High School parking lot so much, but I do. You'd think that vaping and half-dressed teenage girls would make a woman feel grateful to not be a mother, but for some reason, being here with Daisy makes me feel like I haven't completely missed the opportunity.

"Remember, just don't run any red lights, and you'll be fine!" I yell as she opens her car door. I wish I had a bag of Cheetos for her; I'll get some for next time.

The next week, Daisy texts with good news. She passed.

Cold Fries

I hit a stoplight in Hanover and dash off a text message to Susan.

I'm coming home. Another bad date. FML

It's a glorious summer night, windows down, a hint of freshly cut grass in the air. I see now why New Englanders put up with terrible winters, for nights like these. A couple of Dartmouth students saunter through the crosswalk, laughing, drunk with happiness, their whole lives ahead of them. Susan responds within seconds.

Help me. I'm surrounded by Trump supporters.

I speed off in the direction of The Fort, a homey twenty-four-hour diner just off I-89 frequented by truckers. Susan's mother has been admitted to the hospital, and she's waiting for more information. I don't know how Susan has managed to hold it together. Just six months ago at Christmas, Esther joined us at Susan's table for cheesy scalloped potatoes, and now this.

Most of the burly men have lumbered out by the time I arrive a couple of hours before midnight. A few stragglers are sitting at the counter. Susan is alone at a corner booth, wearing colorful cat-eyed spectacles, her iPad within inches of her face.

I slide onto the cushion opposite her. "Any word yet?"

She shakes her head. "Have some of my fries."

You don't have to tell me twice. I squeeze a messy blob of ketchup onto her plate and slather her fries in it. I already know just by looking at them that they are going to be terrible, given their pale white color, but I'm hungry. Still, they're even worse than I thought. Squishy and cold, no soul to them at all.

Sharing fries was something my mother and I did all the time, except we did it at Jib Jab, a hot dog shop just off I-80 in Ohio. We settled into a booth there after Mass on Saturday night. I suffered through plenty of boring sermons for those fries. They were always hot and crispy, and I liked to get mine covered in melted cheese. I craved them after my mother died but couldn't face eating in the restaurant without her. I resorted to the drive-through, but by the time I got home with the fries, they were cold. I popped them in the microwave, but they just came out soggy, kind of like the ones on the plate in front of me right now. I toss a half-eaten fry back on Susan's plate.

Susan hands me a menu. This is my kind of place. Grilled cheese, mozzarella sticks, onion rings, freshly made pies on display. If only I had as many good dating options. "Too bad life isn't like a diner, where you can get anything you want."

"Didn't your date feed you?"

"He made veggie burgers. They weren't very good."

"How did you meet him again?"

"I met him at a bar the night someone else stood me up."

"Did he try and do anything?"

"Do anything?"

"Touch you."

I don't know what's worse: going on bad dates or no dates at all. When I don't date, all I think about is sex. When I go on a bad date, all I can think about is going home to Ronan. Having to answer to Susan doesn't feel good, but it's keeping me honest. I think I'm better off alone. I'd rather be hanging out with Susan and Jake watching *Jeopardy!* than sitting at opposite ends of the couch with a man, hoping maybe I'll actually feel something when I kiss him. Lately, I've been craving companionship, a man's hands on my body. Hot sex, hot fries. I want it all. "He made dinner, then we kissed for a while on his couch."

"That's it?"

"That's it." How is it that I spent so many of my teenage years trying to be good in my parents' basement in the dark, scared of sex. Now I want it, but I can't seem to get it. I don't remember dating being this difficult when I was in my twenties. Getting divorced in my thirties has been weird. Most of the men my age are already married, and the older ones aren't divorced yet.

She wipes her lips with her napkin, then tosses it onto the table. "I don't get it. You've been out with this guy several times now. He hasn't tried anything. It's weird."

She's right. I know it's weird, but who knows what his issues are?

"He shouldn't be able to keep his hands off you. Do you even like him?"

"I don't know yet."

This is a bad sign, I know. I should feel something in my heart or in my loins, but I feel nothing when I'm around him. Even his veggie burger was subpar. How do you mess up a veggie burger? Maybe I shouldn't see him again.

A waitress stops by with the check. Susan checks her phone, then nibbles on a cold fry. Why hasn't she noticed how terrible they are? She always has an opinion on a meal. "I'm still waiting for an update on Mom. The anticipation is terrible. One day she's fine, one day she's not."

"What's wrong this time?"

"I can't keep track anymore. She's just old. Maybe it's finally her time."

I wish I knew what to say to Susan. After my mother's death, I should. I always thought it would be the one redeeming thing about losing her young, that I could help other people through their own grief, but I'm struggling right now to say something original that you wouldn't find on a grocery store greeting card.

"I know you know how this feels . . ." Susan says.

I lean back against the booth. How long ago that was, almost twenty years, and yet how recent it feels.

Was it cancer?

That's what Susan said the first time I told her about my mother. It's actually what most people say. Sometimes, I wish I could say it was. That would be far easier to explain.

I was just about to start my junior year of college in Washington, DC, when I got a call from my father. My mother had gone into the hospital for a gallbladder surgery, a surgery so innocuous that no one even bothered to tell me it was happening, but there were complications following her surgery. She was readmitted to the hospital, then transferred to a better hospital in Cleveland when it looked like she might die.

It was late evening when my father called. I had missed the last flight out, so I got in my car and drove through the night. She was unconscious in the ICU when I arrived, and yet I don't think at that point I fully understood that she could actually die. I thought that everything would be better now that I was home, that my presence could somehow fix her.

A doctor pulled my father and me into a room, sat on the other side of a table, and said that when my mother was at the hospital in Youngstown, she had been given heparin, a common blood thinner, but she ended up being allergic to it, and nobody realized it. There were more complications: a blockage in her superior mesenteric artery, a fistula, bleeding in her upper gastrointestinal tract. In the last few weeks of her life, she developed sepsis and died.

The last book she read before she died was *A Perfect Storm*, and to this day, I cannot think of a better way to describe what happened to her. There's no simple explanation for it, no single word like *cancer* to sum up the hell. I didn't understand how I had wound up with such terrible luck. I couldn't ever remember my mother being sick.

Maybe I'm helping Susan just by being here, by telling her my terrible dating stories, by giving her something to think about that isn't her mother. I always liked that, when my friends talked about their problems. It reminded me that there was a whole other world out there, one that existed outside hospital doors, and maybe one I'd be lucky enough to return to one day.

Susan eats another fry, then slips her iPad into her purse. "My mother's had a good life. We'd all be lucky to live as long as her. You didn't have enough time with your mom. She died too young."

She did. I see that now. The older I get, the more I see how robbed I was. No one should die in their fifties, not when the second half of their life is just beginning.

I wish I had been able to help my mom. She waited a long time before checking out her stomach pain. Earlier that summer, she had come to see me in DC, and I remember telling her to go to the doctor, but she didn't want to. How could I force her? She was my mother, the one who was supposed to know best.

I can't imagine how quiet it will be without Susan and Jake, just like my own house after my mother's death, where I could hear the furnace kick on and off, the pendulums ticking back and forth on my mother's clocks.

"Are you coming home tonight? Need me to let the dogs out?"

"No, that's okay. Jake is home."

Susan places her credit card on the table. She might seem put-together, but I know she's not. Her plate is empty. She's eaten all her cold fries, highly unusual for a woman who once apologized for buying store-bought tzatziki and not making it herself. Susan's mind is somewhere else, with her mother.

We grab our purses and dart outside into a summer rainstorm. "Let me know if there's anything I can do," I say. We hug, which we don't do often. I can feel the soft folds of skin on her back through her thin T-shirt, now moist with raindrops. Susan may have had an extra thirty years with her mother, but she's grieving just like I am. My mother died young; hers will die old. No matter how much time you get, it's never enough.

Taxi Tomato

I think my deodorant stopped working an hour ago. Susan and I are gardening in the backyard, and I'm so tired that I wish she would plant my tomato for me, but I think that defeats the whole purpose of getting your hands dirty. I wipe sweat off my forehead. "This is hard work. I'm ready to call it a day."

"You'll get it!" Susan yells, tossing one of her gardening tools at me. "Use my trowel. It'll go faster."

"How long does it take to grow a tomato anyway? A week?"

"That would be the fastest-growing tomato I've ever heard of."

Earlier today, Susan and I drove to Killdeer Farm across the river in Vermont. It was humid and rainy, a terrible morning to be outside, but it was the only time Susan had available. She's been spending most of her afternoons at the hospital with her mother.

"Do you want perennials or annuals?" Susan asked, plopping fuzzy green plants and herbs into her rickety wagon.

I didn't know the difference between the two, though my mother certainly would have. If only she were still alive to teach me how to do this stuff. We had flower beds all around the yard and green hosta plants lining the perimeter of our white and black Cape Cod house. There was always something blooming around our back deck or the wishing well: daffodils, lilacs, hydrangeas. Everything had its moment in the sun. When one plant died, another bloomed. Her timing was impeccable.

Susan and I ducked into a greenhouse full of tomato plants. There were so many varieties. Soft raindrops tapped on the plastic roof. A tomato called "the taxi" caught my eye. It reminded me of New York City, how so much of my life took place in the back seat of cabs. I took taxis to job interviews and traveled to weddings and doctor's appointments. I shared too many personal details with cab drivers late at night, my cheek resting against a cold window as I tried to stay awake. I did my makeup in taxis and made out with men in the back seat. How lucky I felt late at night, spotting a taxi with its light on, ready to take me home.

I placed a taxi plant in my wagon, then added a basil plant for my frozen pizza, and something called French tarragon because it earned a five-star endorsement from Susan. "Life without French tarragon is not a life worth living," she said, placing one in her wagon.

Back home, Susan demonstrated how to finger a plant so the roots crumbled away from the dirt. "Now you try."

I got down on my knees and filled a heavy pot to the brim with dirt, then carved out a section for all my herbs. It's funny to think that I used to try to distance myself as much as possible from my surroundings in New York City, the noise, the pollution, but here I'm immersed in everything, even dirt. The one thing I could use, however, is another pot.

"I have one you could borrow, but if you want it, you have to get it," Susan said.

"Where is it? The garage?"

"Jake's shed."

Jake's shed. His man cave, where dust-covered dog crates house spiders, and lawn tools hang from the wooden walls, sharp enough to decapitate someone in one quick swipe. Susan points to a table covered in cobwebs. "It's under there."

"Hell no."

"Oh, it's not that bad."

"If it's not that bad, then why can't you get it for me?"

"I have bad knees."

"I thought CBD fixed everything?"

"I can't get under the table."

"You mean the cobweb-covered table?"

"Do you want it or not? It's free . . ."

Free. My favorite word. I pull the pot out from under the table, as if I'm Indiana Jones entering an Egyptian tomb, and scrape out crunchy autumn leaves from the bottom. An angry daddy longlegs climbs out and scurries off.

Susan peers into the pot. "I can't believe there aren't any dead mice inside."

I can't believe we aren't at the hospital getting me a rabies shot. "Now what?"

"We wait."

Waiting. Something I'm terrible at. But I have no choice. In the coming days after I plant my taxi tomato, I return twice a day with the hose, sprinkling the garden beds with a soft fizz that curves in the morning and evening sunlight. I come up with a list of foods I will pair with my taxi tomato: an egg-and-cheese sandwich, a spinach salad, a simple mozzarella-and-basil number.

Most afternoons, Susan calls from the hospital to check in. Esther is in intensive care, the way my mother was. I know I should stop by the hospital to check in on Susan and Esther. It sounds like Esther is getting worse. I went the other day, but practically everyone else in the family had gone then, and with only a few visitors allowed inside at a time, I offered up my spot in line. I left the hospital that day feeling relieved. I didn't want to cry in front of anyone. I know it won't matter that Susan's mother isn't my mother or that nearly twenty years have passed since I was in that hospital room. It'll be like reliving it all over again.

"I'll swing by," I say when Susan calls, though I don't know if that's true. "How are you?"

"Terrible. How's your tomato doing?"

"No tomato yet." Susan likes to ask about my gardening exploits. Sometimes it seems like that's the only diversion she has. She certainly can't ask about my love life. Nothing happening there.

"It's a hot one today. Are you watering?"

"I am, but nothing is happening. Maybe I'm doing something wrong."

"It'll come. Be patient. Just wait until you taste your first tomato! Nothing tops it. Except for maybe sex."

Sex. Who knows when I'll have that again. Maybe the universe will do me a solid and give me both at the same time.

"I got your mail for you today," I say, realizing that I'm just like Jake now, looking through their mail, the way he does to me. "When are you coming home? Do you want to hang out on the porch tonight?"

"I don't think so. We'll be home after dark."

Until she stopped coming home at a normal time, I hadn't realized how much I depend on Susan for company. Sometimes, when I let Ronan out for the last pee of the night, I wander out by the garden beds and tilt my head back to take in the stars. Summer in New England feels romantic, a strange time to be alone. There's a faint wetness in the night air. It really is the best time of year. The trees lining the road are so lush and full that you can't even see the house from the road anymore. It's so beautiful that I've almost forgotten how bad winter was. In the same way, I don't think as much anymore about how unhappy I was in New York.

In the coming weeks, I continue to water both my plants and Susan's, with no idea how long it'll be until Susan comes home or at what moment our tomatoes will ripen. I know it'll be soon because the vines on my tomato plant have started to spiral skyward like beanstalks in a children's book. There are no actual tomatoes, but the vines are so thick and heavy that they start to bend over, and I have to use clothespins to attach them to Jake's bamboo sticks.

One morning, I wake up to a text from Susan. Her mother died. I've known this day would come, but it's still hard to accept.

I get out of bed and let Ronan out into the yard. It seems like such a strange time to die: July, life in full bloom, the birds gossiping about an exceptionally beautiful sunrise.

The grass is wet with dew, the sunlight already sneaking through the white pines, the type of morning my mother would have loved. It always seemed cruel to lose her when I did, in October. Fall was her favorite season. I remember driving to and from the hospital to see her, marveling at the color of the leaves.

As each year passed, I dreaded the anniversary of her death, but over time, the splendor of the season stepped in to comfort me, so much so that I began looking forward to the arrival of fall. I didn't even notice it was happening. It was a gradual change, like the leaves themselves falling. Now, I'm so captivated by the swirl of color around me come October that I can't seem to imagine my mother dying at any other time. I know that the glory of summer will comfort Susan on the anniversary of her mother's death, the way autumn leaves do for me.

That's one thing I love about living here in New England, how immersed I am in nature and the seasons. In the city, the only hint I had of that was catching a glimpse of the moon between buildings when I took Ronan out for his final walk of the night. I marked the days by calendar alerts on my phone, not like I do now, by the golden color of the fall leaves, the smell of the warm summer air when I step outside, or the ripening of a tomato. Time feels more precious here. I'm more aware of each passing day. It's hard to believe, but soon I will have been living here for an entire year.

I pick up the garden hose and turn on the spigot. And that's when I see it: a small flash of yellow in my pot. My first tomato is ready. Perfect timing.

MATING SEASON

There's a Fly in Your Drink

Maybe my date Andrew has allergies. Maybe he has something in his eye. Maybe I should stop making excuses. A crying middle-aged man can't really be misread.

Andrew is sitting across the picnic table from me, dabbing his eyes with a stained coffee napkin. A fall breeze tries to whisk his napkin away. He tucks it under his saucer.

"Are you crying because of your divorce?" I ask, though I know he is. We've been talking about Andrew's children and the house that he and his ex just sold. I can't say "ex-wife" because they're still married. What am I doing here with this guy? He's clearly not ready for a relationship.

Andrew leans in and picks a woolly bug off my arm. "These are the ones you need to worry about." Guess he's lived here long enough that he can tell the difference between good bugs and bad ones.

A young girl with pigtails swirls a Hula-Hoop around her hips. Cedar Circle Farm seemed like a great spot for a date, and it was, until Andrew started crying. There was no alcohol to muddle anything, just lattes with foam-shaped hearts in teacups, gourds galore, and a barn cat rubbing up against a tree.

This farm, which sells coffee and pastries, is one of my favorite spots to work. It has great juju. When I come here to write, I feel like I've made it, even when the Wi-Fi stops working. This is what I wanted for my life when I left New York City, though I couldn't see it at the time. Cedar Circle was one of the first places I rode my bike to, and I've been coming here ever since. Now I've messed it all up by bringing a date here. This will always be the picnic table where I went on a date with the man who cried. I hope the young girl with the Hula-Hoop doesn't ask Andrew why he's crying. Just wait until you get older, honey.

I worried maybe it was too soon to date Andrew when we met a couple nights ago at Pine. Eleanor had come up from New York for the weekend and we had gone out for a drink after a full day of leaf-peeping. There was a chill in the air that night. It felt like we had walked into a ski lodge; a shoulder-to-shoulder crowd huddled by the fireplace under the ceiling's thick wooden beams. Two seats suddenly became available at the bar.

"Perfect timing!" Eleanor said. "Grab them and order us some drinks."

I pulled out the empty barstool on the right. Eleanor ushered me to the left.

"Sit here instead," she whispered, a step ahead of me, making sure I sat next to Andrew. He was absolutely my type. He was wearing quirky glasses—blue with rectangular frames—and a maroon Patagonia fleece, which gave him a college professor vibe. A fresh earthy scent, as if he had just showered with the pines, floated into my airspace, then straight to my loins when I slid onto the wooden barstool next to him.

When our cocktails arrived, Andrew leaned close to inspect my glass. "There's a fly in your drink," he said.

Impossible, I thought. But when I peered closely at my cocktail, I saw that he was right. There was a small fruit fly slurping up my drink. I fished it out with my finger. Eleanor balked. She'd been a good sport playing outdoors with me but drew the line at contaminated drinks. "Gross. Let's get you a new one."

"I'll take another cider," Andrew said. "Bug-free, please." He laughed. "So, what is that you're drinking? Or that you were drinking . . ."

The bartender slid a new, bug-free cocktail for me across the mahogany bar.

"They call it a Northern Standard. It's like a Manhattan, but better," I said, reciting what the bartender said to me at Pine a year ago when I came here with Susan and Jake my first night in town. One sip of the Northern Standard and all of the stress and uncertainty of starting over dissipated into a warm fuzzy feeling. New town, new cocktail, new life.

"What's in it?" Andrew asked.

"Rye whiskey, sweet vermouth, and bitters," I said, sliding a plump maraschino cherry into my drink, dripping red juice onto the bottom of the coupe glass. "Try it."

I slid the drink in his direction and started to wonder what his astrological sign was. Confident enough to be out on his own talking to strangers. Aries?

He lifted my glass to taste it. "Wow! That's really good. My father loved Manhattans."

"Loved?"

"He died a few years ago."

"Oh. I'm sorry. Well, I bet he would have loved this drink."

"Actually, I bet he had one. He used to come to this bar when he visited town."

I couldn't figure it out. Who was this man? How had I never seen him in town before? Maybe his wife died, and he was back on the market. Susan had told me I should read the obituaries if I ever wanted to get a date around here.

Andrew took off his maroon fleece, revealing a gray T-shirt, perfectly coordinated with his hair color.

Eleanor leaned toward us, a glass of prosecco dangling in her hand. "What do you do for work?"

"I bet you work at Dartmouth," I said. "You're dressed the part."

"I run an affordable housing agency."

"How come I've never seen you here?"

"I never went out when I was married. I'm getting divorced."

Jackpot.

Eleanor raised her glass. "Welcome to the club! We're divorcées."

"Aren't you a little young for that?"

"God bless you," Eleanor said. "Divorcées come in all ages and sizes. You shouldn't discriminate. How far along are you?"

"We just separated," Andrew replied.

I winced. "Stage one. You definitely need to be drinking something stronger. Is your wife still in town?"

"Right down the street. We sold the house, and I have my own apartment, but I can't move in for a few more weeks. I may not even stay in town anyway. I'm interviewing for jobs elsewhere."

"I left town too. I moved here from New York City a year ago." If getting divorced felt like hell in New York, what would it feel like in a town where everyone knows each other? "It must be terrible getting divorced in a small town."

"You have no idea. Half the people in this bar probably think my ex and I are still together."

"God, that's awkward," I said. "How long were you married?"

Andrew laughed. "Twenty-five years."

"Fucking hell, that's a lifetime," Eleanor said.

I had always felt terrible that my marriage only lasted a few years, but maybe that wasn't so bad after all. Maybe the only thing worse than a short marriage is a long one.

"God, is it that bad?" Andrew asked. "Excuse me while I down my drink."

"You haven't even started dating yet. It's hell," I said. "Actually, I bet you won't have a problem." I inched closer to him. "Okay, I have to ask. When's your birthday?"

"June 5. Why?"

"You're a Gemini! I'm a Gemini."

Imagine that. I never dated a Gemini. Two Geminis, the sign of the twins. Would that be like a foursome?

By the time the bartender yelled last call, I couldn't believe how late it was. I had never closed down Pine before. I swiped Andrew's phone off the bar, programmed my number in it, and shoved it back in his hand. Eleanor pulled me out the door. "I hope you like dogs!" I yelled.

"I do! I used to have a Lab, but my ex got her!"

"Good luck with your divorce!" Eleanor yelled. "You've got her number now!"

It had been a year since I moved to Hanover. Maybe I was right to stick it out. Maybe my luck was finally changing. At least that's what I thought until Andrew started crying at this picnic table. He's worse than stage one. He's stage zero. I can't believe I washed my hair and put on eyeliner to have the morning end this way.

"Listen, I think we should just call it a day. I don't know if you're ready for dating yet." I certainly am. I've been alone for years and have had plenty of time to think about what I want. "Should we get going?"

"Wait," Andrew says, placing his hand on mine. "You can't go already. We just got here. God, I've really blown it, haven't I?" He crumbles his napkin into his pocket. "I'm sorry for being a bad date. I've been so overwhelmed lately. I don't know what I'm doing."

I don't want to tell him he has a long way to go, but I don't know what else to say. I just want to get out of here. "I need to do some work."

"Oh, well, let me carry your teacup for you at least. I guess I should probably head to the office . . ."

We drop off our empty teacups at a little barn, then stroll to our cars in the gravel parking lot. It's a bright fall day. Pots are overflowing with mums so big they could topple over. Voluptuous pumpkins are strewn across the field, leaves in their full autumnal splendor: orange, yellow, and burgundy.

"Well, thanks for the coffee," I say, though I don't want to bother with small talk. I just want to go home and burrow my head into Ronan's chest.

"Wait." Andrew pulls me close and kisses me. It's surprising and still somehow so smooth that I don't have time to protest, but I don't want to either. Is there something here worth exploring? A screaming child runs past. Could the timing of this get any worse? This kiss, Andrew's divorce, his crying. A few bikers are staring at us.

"Sorry, I know that was kind of forward, but I couldn't help myself," Andrew says. "I hope the kids didn't see that. Can we try this date again another time?"

I don't know. Can I take a gamble on Andrew? There's a good chance this might end in heartbreak, but knowing what Andrew is going through makes it a little easier for me to take a leap. Andrew's heart is broken, but that also means it's open. He'll probably come out okay on the other side like I did, but getting there is going to be a little bumpy.

"How about I text you later," I say.

Andrew grins. "I promise I won't cry twice." He dabs his eyes with a tissue and stuffs it back inside his pocket.

Andrew is what my father would call a "dog," short for *underdog*. Definitely a longshot.

Cosmic Trash

I'm trying to count numbers on mailboxes, but Susan is driving too fast. "Slow down. I want to take a photo of Andrew's house for Eleanor."

Susan and I have Googled Andrew's address online, and we've gone out this afternoon to drive past his house. Basically, we're stalking him. It's something I did all the time in high school with Eleanor, drive past the homes of boys we had crushes on. It didn't accomplish much back then, and I don't know what I'm hoping to get out of it today.

"This is so exciting! You finally have someone in your life!" Susan says. She dons sunglasses, then glances in the rearview mirror. "So I won't be recognized. Everyone knows me in town from the computer store. Do you have sunglasses?"

"I don't need them. No one knows me."

"Well, they're gonna know who you are once you take a married man as your boyfriend!"

I roll down my window. "I wouldn't call Andrew my boyfriend. We went on a date, and he cried. Don't you think that's a red flag?"

"It means he's sensitive. That's just what you need. No more men from the British Isles for you."

"You're still driving too fast. We're getting close. Slow down."

We pass a fenced-in Cape and another home with an American flag and a manicured, leaf-free lawn, then round a tight corner on a quiet street.

Susan taps the brakes. "Does Andrew like modern homes? Did you tell him you live in a home designed by the famous Hunter architects?"

"Keep going . . . nearly there."

"He works in housing. Surely, he knows about them. You can't date him if he doesn't know who the Hunters are and doesn't have good taste in architecture and—"

"Stop! There it is!"

Susan pulls to the side of the road, a quiet two-lane drive, shady with trees. I hope no one sees us.

"I thought this was his house," I say. "I've always loved this one!"

Andrew's home is a two-story modern abode, painted slate gray, with solar panels on the roof and floor-to-ceiling windows.

"Well, at least we know he has good taste," Susan says, turning off the engine.

"Should we keep driving?"

"I think we're safe. There's no one around."

The front door is painted bright yellow—quite the statement, like Susan's house, except hers is lime green. There is one flaw at Andrew's house: a tilted mailbox, like ours was in Ohio from too many people hitting it at the edge of the driveway.

Crispy fall leaves flutter across the yard, but I know no one is coming to pick them up. No one cares about them right now. That house is divorce territory.

"I wonder what kind of furniture they have?" Susan asks. She slides off her sunglasses. "I can sort of see some nice stuff in there."

"He showed me a few photos. I think they shopped at a place called Design Within Reach?" I shrug. "Never heard of it . . ."

"He's your boyfriend within reach! That's what we can call him behind his back . . . BWR."

Susan loves acronyms and nicknames. She hasn't let up at all with this idea of Andrew becoming my boyfriend. I don't know why she's so certain that this is going to all work out.

"He's not *really* within reach. He's technically still married, and he's interviewing for jobs in California and South Carolina."

"I wonder if Andrew and his wife ever came into our store? I bet they did. I'll ask him when you bring him around. What should I make for dinner when he visits? What does he like to drink?"

"He was drinking cider when I met him, but I think I switched him to Manhattans."

Yesterday when I told Susan about my date with Andrew, she pulled out her iPad, inserted Andrew's name into Google, pulled up his LinkedIn profile, and clicked on it before I had a chance to stop her.

"Wait!" I yelled. "You can't use LinkedIn! Now he'll be able to tell you've looked at his profile. I don't want him to know I'm stalking him. No one wants to date a stalker."

She spun her iPad around, showing me a business profile shot of Andrew in a gray suit and a pink tie. "He's good-looking!"

"Why do you sound shocked?"

"I don't know. He has hair. I thought you only liked bald men."

I peered at her phone. "You're already friends on LinkedIn. How did that happen?"

Maybe Andrew came into Susan and Jake's computer store and bought his son a new Mac, never imagining for a second that one day years from now he would be trying to woo the woman living in Susan's basement. Maybe I passed him on the street the day Jack and I picked up Ronan, when I was running back to the rental car with coffees in my hand, just before we found the valet ticket that had the name *Ronan* on it.

"This is weird," Susan said. "I know everyone in town, but I don't recognize him. I think we met in Rotary. He and his wife bid on some paintings."

"Probably the ones hanging in his house right now. He's not even officially divorced yet. His life is a mess."

I remember when I was in that stage, how confused I was. One night, I was out at a bar back in New York, and I started talking to a cute architect, who asked me if I had ever been married. It was such a direct question and one that I wasn't ready to answer, so I lied. And yet, my divorce was one of the first topics Andrew and I covered. I felt comfortable with him, like there was a mutual understanding between us. What do you call it when your baggage aligns with someone else's? Cosmic trash?

Another car passes by. A teenager in the driver's seat stares a little too long at us. 1 inch lower.

"Maybe we should get out of here," I say. "The neighbors are going to think we're pedophiles, and your car is too obvious. It has that Glen of Imaal terrier decal on the side."

"Oh, they'd never put it together. Didn't you say they have a Lab? Lab people don't know anything about terriers!"

Sitting here in front of Andrew's house makes me think about the future, how long I'll be living in Susan's house, and if I'll ever have my own home one day. I hope so. I've been a renter ever since my mom died. It always felt impossible to own a home in New York City because of how expensive it was to live there. How fun it would be to decorate a home the way I want and have a family of my own. Maybe Susan and Jake will live nearby. Susan will probably try to stage all the rooms, and Jake will probably tell me that I'm doing my recycling wrong. Wonder if they'd babysit? Maybe I could have more dogs!

Susan pats my knee, rattling me from my daydream. "I'm happy for you. This is all great news."

I hope she's right. I wonder if Andrew might be relationship material or, at the very least, someone to have fun with until he skips town. It feels like the timing is finally right for me. My divorce was finalized two years ago. I don't know what the future holds, but I finally feel content with where I'm at, even if I'm living in Susan's basement.

For so long, I wished that my divorce had never happened in the first place, but lately I've been thinking about the good things that have come from it. I'm so much happier here than I was in New York, doing my own thing with my freelance writing, hopping in my car to cover assignments for the newspaper at a moment's notice. What a crazy thing I did moving up here, but so far, it's actually been working out. Sure, there have been hard moments, but even so, I don't regret my decision. How is it possible that something I didn't want to happen directly led to something that I did want to happen?

Another car approaches from the opposite direction with a woman behind the wheel. I duck.

"Do you think that was his ex-wife?" I ask.

Susan shifts the car into drive. "Nope, not her."

"How would you know?"
"I've already looked her up on Facebook for you."
Of course she has.

Silent G for $200

My phone vibrates with a text. It's Andrew.

Which door should I use?

Good question. In the last two weeks, he's been using the back entrance by the garage to get to my downstairs apartment. Each time he's showed up at the house, there's been something in his hand: a suitcase with work clothes or a painting from the house that he and his ex sold.

Use the front!

Going through the front door is a big deal, an acknowledgment that we're something, though I don't know what yet. It feels like we're in a relationship, but Andrew hasn't removed the possibility of leaving town. In the meantime, I've been losing space in my medicine cabinet. Inch by inch, row by row, Andrew lines the rickety shelves with deodorant and shaving cream so that he can go straight to work from my place.

Tonight, Andrew is coming over for an evening of *Jeopardy!*. This will be the true test to see if he fits in here with our little twisted pseudo-family.

I want this night to go well. I washed my hair, applied tinted ChapStick, and even put on jeans instead of leggings. But I'm worried about Susan blowing it for me with her nosiness. She asked plenty of inappropriate questions when I was going through my divorce: "How much alimony did you get?" "Have you had sex with anyone else yet?" "How much does your lawyer charge an hour?" Surely, she will subject Andrew, who is going through his own divorce, to the same interrogation. I just want her to act normal.

How did I do this back in high school? If I were introducing a date to my parents, my father would have answered the door without a shirt on, then excused himself to call his bookie to place a bet on the Browns game. My mother would have introduced herself, then warned my date about our septic system. I was always mortified, but there was no way around it.

Andrew is going to walk in any minute. Where will he sit? I'm in my usual spot, on the couch with Rooney and Picabo jostling for a spot on my lap. Jake shuffles out the door to get firewood, then dumps another log on the fire.

An alert from Apple flashes across my phone. My screen time rose 40 percent from the week before, thanks to Andrew.

Susan picks up her iPad. She's been researching at-home hair colors. "Did Andrew stay the night? I saw his car in the driveway at half past three this morning."

This might go worse than I thought. "You've got to stop spying on me!"

The other morning, after Andrew spent the night, I couldn't figure out how Susan knew to call me the second Andrew's car pulled off. I was standing in the driveway when I picked up her phone call.

"Is this another butt-dial?"

"What happened? You seem unhappy."

"Where are you?" I turned around. A faint shadow in the upstairs window disappeared from view. "Oh my God! Don't tell me you were watching us say goodbye from the window?"

I imagined her ranking all my actions. No smiling? Minus ten points. No kissing? Minus fifty points. I should've known she would spy on me. This was, after all, the first time in a year I had brought a man back to my apartment.

"You didn't kiss Andrew goodbye," she said. "Why not?"

It wasn't really any of her business, but I knew she'd keep on nagging me for information. "Don't worry. He was in a rush. We're fine."

"Is he good in bed? Remember, women should always come first."

"Oh my God," I said through laughter. Outrageous, though Bridget probably would have asked the same thing. "It all felt very natural. He was very attentive."

"Fantastic! How was the mattress? You know, it has good juju. Jake and I made our kids on that bed."

Gross. "I wish you hadn't told me that."

"Why didn't you kiss Andrew goodbye just now? You looked sad."

"I guess I'm just scared. What if I fall in love, and it all goes away again?"

"New love is scary, but you're moving forward. Don't worry, I was watching you! Come upstairs and tell me everything."

Was she watching me when Jack and I pulled out of the driveway with Ronan? Was she judging me then too? Probably. She must have missed something because she was as shocked as anyone that we didn't last, devastated even. Surprising, especially considering that she used to be a divorce lawyer. Of all people, wouldn't she have been the one to spot a marriage in trouble?

Maybe I should have waited a little longer to bring Andrew around for *Jeopardy!*. But if he's leaving town anyway, what do I have to lose?

"So, is it official? Is he your boyfriend?" Susan asks, as we wait for Andrew to come inside. "I didn't want to say anything, but if you guys are shacking up already . . ."

"If you didn't *want* to say anything, why are you saying anything? And what were you doing up that early anyway?"

"That's when I get up to pee."

"We both do," Jake says. "Though I usually have to go a little earlier, around two thirty."

"And you just happened to wander into the spare bedroom to look out the window to see if his car was in the driveway?"

"I needed to make sure he hasn't left you for Chico," she replies.

Chico! Ugh. Unfortunately, I'm not the only one who wants Andrew. A housing agency in Chico, California, wants Andrew to move there and build housing for people who lost their homes in the wildfires. I feel a little selfish that I want him all for myself while other people lost their homes, but not selfish enough that I'd ever tell him to take the job.

"If he leaves you for Chico, I'll kill him," Jake says.

Susan takes a quick hit from her vape. "If he leaves you, I'll make those cheesy julienne potatoes you like."

The downstairs door swishes open. Rooney and Picabo rush off to the landing. Andrew's footsteps shuffle up the stairs. He has a goofy smile plastered across his face, the same one I have on mine, I can tell, by the way Susan looks at us and sighs.

"Hello, you," he says, removing his gloves and jacket.

Jake spins around in his chair. "Hey, Andrew! Come on in! You're just in time for *Jeopardy!*. Wanna stay for dinner?"

Wow, he's already getting the royal treatment. Andrew slides in next to me on the couch. I hope there aren't any political categories tonight. Andrew is so into politics that he once told me he considers Election Day more fun than his birthday.

Andrew points to Rooney. "That one's Romney, right? The white one?"

"Susan would never, ever name a dog after Mitt Romney," I say.

"Shhhh, all of you!" Susan yells. Alex Trebek takes his position. Categories flash across the screen. We hold our breath.

Historic Trios.

Uh-oh. Andrew was a history major at Bowdoin. I'm screwed.

Asian Geography.

Andrew island-hopped over there after college.

Scorpios.

I can't believe my luck! An astrology category! "You guys all are toast."

"Quiet!" Susan says. A clue flashes across the television screen.

In World War I the nucleus of the Allies was the Triple Entente: Great Britain, Russia & this country.

"France!" Andrew shouts.

Correct!

"BOOM!" he yells.

"Shit," Susan says.

In the early 20th century, the three top-of-the-White Star Line ocean liners were the Olympic, the Britannic & this doomed one.

Oh, that's easy it's the—

"Titanic!" Andrew yells. "BOOM!"

Susan shoots me a look. Time for another drink.

We breathe a sigh of relief during the commercial break. I had some wins. I remembered the lyrics to the Mister Rogers' theme song and correctly guessed that Monet was a Scorpio.

Susan got a few answers right, but I wonder if she's annoyed that I brought Andrew. She picks up her iPad again. Maybe she's fact-checking all of tonight's clues.

"Andrew, you look so familiar," she says. "Have we met before? In Rotary, maybe?"

"Sounds right. My ex and I bought a painting at an auction you were running. There was another time too. I came into your computer store with my family once."

"What did you buy?" Jake asks. "I hope we gave you good customer service!"

"I always liked your ads," Andrew says. "That photo of Jake smiling on the side of the bus was great."

"That was my idea!" Susan says. "Betsy told me you're going through a divorce. How's it going?"

"Susan!" I yell. "Maybe he doesn't want to talk about that."

"It's okay. It's actually nice to be around people who know what I'm going through."

"Oh, we get it, all right," Jake says, laughing. "I'm divorced myself."

"Have you separated your finances yet?" Susan asks.

"No."

Susan tosses a small notepad off the end table in Andrew's direction. "Take notes."

I shoot Susan a look that says *stop*. It's the same look she gives me when she catches me feeding her dogs from my plate. Maybe I should have done what I did in high school, whisk my boyfriend down into the basement to avoid any more embarrassing interactions. I guess not much has changed since then, given that I literally live in a basement now. I suppose I could have avoided all this by sneaking Andrew in through the back door to my apartment, but I actually wanted Susan and Jake to meet him.

She leans back in her chair. "Do you have a lawyer yet?"

"I don't."

"You don't? Well, when were you planning on getting one? You need a real bulldog. You know, I used to represent men in divorce cases. Never lost a case in my whole career. Too bad I'm retired. I could have cleaned up for you."

"We're going to use a mediator. It'll be fine."

"I used a mediator, and it was still terrible," I say. "Every divorce is terrible."

Back from a commercial break. *Double Jeopardy!* is starting. "Turn it up!" Susan yells.

"I'll take '*Silent G*' for $200," a contestant says.

California is no stranger to these dry spells.

"Drought!" Jake yells.

"California . . ." Susan mutters. "Andrew, you're not really going to move there, are you?"

Now *this* I want to talk about. What is Andrew going to do? I've never dated someone who was simultaneously investigating an exit strategy, but it doesn't feel right for me to tell him to stay here.

"You'd be a fool to leave our girl," Susan says.

Andrew inches closer to me. "Believe me, I know."

If he knows, then why is he leaving? Andrew's indecisiveness bothers me, but, having been there myself, I understand. I guess I'd rather have a blocked drain from his whiskers than an empty bed. "You should cancel your interview," I say.

"You don't want me to go?" Andrew asks.

I squeeze his hand. "I like having you here. How can you leave all this fun!"

"Well, I certainly wouldn't mind getting closer to you while I'm still here," he says. "I know I'm complicated, but I'm pretty head over heels for you."

How is this all going to turn out? Best-case scenario? Andrew sticks around for a few more months. That would give us more time together. Then again, I couldn't imagine staying in New York City for a man, so why am I expecting him to do that? This actually feels a lot like *Jeopardy!*. Tough questions, but that doesn't mean you should stop playing the game.

Andrew creams us all in *Final Jeopardy!*, then stays for dinner for more of Susan's interrogation.

"Let's sit at the table," Susan says, handing me a basket of warm bread. Nothing would make me happier than doing this the entire winter, playing *Jeopardy!* with my surrogate parents and my married boyfriend and eating so much bread that I have to unbutton my jeans so that I can breathe properly.

I corner Susan by the sink. "Well ... what do you think? Do you like him? Are you mad you lost?"

"Of course not. I thrive on competition. He's good. Bring him back tomorrow."

If Chico doesn't get in my way, I will.

Crazy Talk

The psychic closes her eyes, pauses, then blinks them open again. "Your mother is telling me that she has a message for you."

This is unbelievable. In all my time trying magical candles, tarot readings, and moon ceremonies, I never had anyone say that my mother was trying to contact me, not once in eighteen years.

"Your mother says, 'Thanks for the grandchildren.'"

Well, this has to be a scam. I don't even have children. Plus, my mother was far too feisty for something generic like "Thanks for the grandchildren." She would have been far more likely to say, "Sorry for all those times I embarrassed you in front of your boyfriends talking about our septic system." Or, "I wish I had bought you that Jeep Wrangler you always wanted." Or, "Twelve years of Catholic school, and you can't go to church on the weekends?"

I brought Andrew here with me to a psychic fair at our town hall, across the street from our morning coffee and bagel place. At my suggestion, we wandered in to mingle with the witches, crystal healers, and paranormal investigators who were waiting and willing to read our tarot cards and channel the deceased for $20.

Andrew is at a nearby table, with all the other Muggles in an airy open room that probably dates back at least a hundred years, maybe more. The murmur of conversation floats around the room, but I can't hear what he's saying. I try to read his body language, but I can't tell from the back of his Red Sox hat if he's getting scammed too. I need this psychic to tell me what's going to happen in our relationship, but she's gone all crazy with the grandkids talk.

Andrew picked his psychic with little thought, whereas I inspected each psychic's specialties, photos, and credentials. Clearly, I have chosen wrong today in this episode of psychic speed-dating where I have fifteen minutes, now five minutes, to figure out my future. For a moment, I allow myself to entertain the possibility that my mother is trying to communicate with me from the other side. She did have a fantastic sense of humor and often expressed her love toward me with teasing and sarcasm. Is it possible that she is joking with me from the other side? Upset that I am thirty-eight and haven't given her grandchildren yet? Or perhaps I am so desperate to feel her presence that I am reading into something that isn't true.

I know one thing that is certain: I am running out of time to have children. I had always wondered if I had spent so much of my adult life confused about whether to become a mother because I lost mine at such a young age.

The psychic across the table from me awaits my response. Maybe I should lie to see how wild this can get? Would she pick up on it?

"I don't have children."

The psychic grins, then leans forward in her chair. "Not yet, you don't."

"Come on. Do you really see children in my future?"

"I do—two!"

This woman is all crazy talk. All I have right now are four eggs on ice from my attempts at egg-freezing two years ago and a boyfriend who's going through a divorce.

"Do you want kids?" I remember Andrew asking in the car on one of our first dates. It was nighttime and raining so hard that the windshield wipers were springing back and forth as if trying to match my wild heartbeat. It was just a question, but it brought up so much for me: my mother, my marriage, my frozen eggs. Children are supposed to be a symbol of the future, but to me, they also symbolize loss, of life not going according to plan.

"I don't know if children are in my future," I said. "But I have four eggs on ice from a round of egg-freezing I did when I was thirty-six."

"But would you like to have them?"

He shifted into another lane, then turned down the radio.

I admired how direct he was, his curiosity about what I wanted. "I don't know if I'll ever use my eggs, but I like knowing they're there." I didn't mention that I had thought about children enough to know that if I ever had a daughter, I would name her Millie, after my mother.

"Well, don't rule me out," Andrew said. "If you decide you want kids. I know I'd be an old dad, but if you want them, let's talk about it."

This surprised me. Andrew already had children from his first marriage. I never thought he'd want to do it again.

"I think you'd make a great mother," he said.

No one had ever said that to me before, but I liked hearing it, even if Andrew was basing his decision solely on the way I spoiled Ronan. I believed him when he said it, though I had nothing in my life to show for it except for the knowledge that my mother had been a great mother too.

A bell rings. Time's up with the psychic. "Any last questions?" she asks. The room begins to empty out.

Oh, how I wish I could slow down time. I wish Andrew wasn't looking for jobs elsewhere, that he wasn't going through a divorce that makes him want to skip town, but if he weren't going through a divorce, I guess we wouldn't be here right now. Fifteen minutes passed so quickly. I glance at Andrew, then lean in toward the psychic. "That guy over there ... we're dating ... it's still new. He's going through a divorce. Great guy, but his life is messy. I don't know where we're going to end up."

It occurs to me that knowing the end would take away some of the fun. What I want is that feeling I had when I walked into Pine and met Andrew for the first time, a happy surprise. I couldn't have planned it better if I tried.

The psychic turns to look at him, then spins back around, smiling. "You have two roads. Whichever road you take, you'll be fine."

I don't even have time to ask her what's down each road because Andrew appears, grinning. "My psychic told me that I'm going to win a million dollars! You should stick with me!" He laughs.

The psychic slips me her business card. At least I know one person who isn't leading me on: Andrew. I've known this since the day I decided to tell him that I had multiple sclerosis. He didn't know anything about the disease. He listened to my whole story: the routine eye doctor appointment that led to a same-day MRI across town, how I learned to give myself shots, the relapse I had several years ago, the once-a-month hospital infusions I have now. I knew he would Google it the minute he left. I knew how scary the disease looked on the Internet because I had read up on it myself. Telling Andrew was the soonest I had ever told a man about my illness, but something about it just seemed right. We didn't talk about it for the rest of the day, but the next afternoon, Andrew showed up at my apartment with a bouquet of soft pink roses and red dahlias.

They smelled like spring, of new possibilities to be had, Susan's flowers pushing up through the hard, mucky soil, determined to see the sun. At first, I thought it was a romantic gesture, that thing you do at the beginning of a relationship to woo someone over, but then I realized it was more than that. Being vulnerable with him about my illness had taken our relationship to a whole other level.

"I'm all in," he said.

Those three words were his way of saying he had heard everything I said. He knew my illness was unpredictable. I could relapse and end up in a wheelchair. I could lose my vision again. He could be burdened for the rest of his life as my caregiver.

Nothing is certain in life, but Andrew didn't mind then, and he doesn't mind now. That's one thing I know I really like about him. If it feels right, he shows up. He did the same thing today. Any straight, middle-aged man who would willingly come with me to a psychic fair on a Saturday afternoon is absolutely someone I want to get to know better.

"Let's go get some lunch," he says.

As we walk away from the table, I wonder if I've actually been visited by my mother in some weird way. I feel as ready as I've ever been to take the leap. Maybe crazy talk isn't all that crazy if it gets you thinking.

"So, you haven't told me yet what she said," Andrew says. "What's your future hold?"

You, I think.

Just One Night

Someone's phone is ringing, but it's not mine. It's coming from a dark corner in the hotel room. Is the front desk calling, asking us to tone down the sex? Maybe it's Andrew's phone.

"We weren't loud, were we?"

The ringing stops. Andrew rolls toward me in bed.

"There," I say. "It started again. Do you hear that?"

He sits up and rubs his eyes. "That's not my phone."

Uh-oh. That means the phone can only belong to one other person: Andrew's friend Mark, who died in our presence a few hours ago.

Earlier tonight, I was at home with Susan when Andrew showed up. "Come with me to Boston for the night," he said. His friend Mark was in a rehab facility recovering from alcoholism, and Andrew wanted company on the drive.

"Go," Susan said. "We'll watch Ronan."

I was surprised Susan didn't object. Usually, her response to having to babysit Ronan went something like, "Oh sure, what's one more dog to watch when you have four?" Or, "Can't you take him with you?" Or, "He's so lazy that I have to throw a million treats on the ground to get him off the bed!"

On the two-hour drive to Boston in a rainstorm, Andrew told me everything I needed to know. Mark was one of his closest friends. He had relapsed from alcohol so many times over the last few years that Mark's own family had given up on him. Andrew stepped in as Mark's healthcare proxy, having known him ever since law school.

"I wasn't that great of a student. I even failed the bar the first time,"

Andrew said, switching lanes as the windshield wipers worked overtime. "I struggled. Mark got me through it."

How could that be? Andrew was a whiz at *Jeopardy!*. I thought of him as someone who could open the newspaper and talk about anything.

The elevator doors slid open when we arrived at the rehab facility. A lone nurse pointed down the hall to the last room on the left. I wasn't sure what I was going to say, how I was going to introduce myself, but I didn't need to worry about that because Mark was unconscious. He was propped up with pillows in a hospital bed, eyes closed, his breathing heavy, in tune with whirring hospital equipment.

"Mark?" Andrew said, trying to rouse him. We slipped off our wet coats and draped them over a chair. A few drops of water fell onto the floor.

"Mark, I'm here," Andrew said. "And I brought my friend Betsy."

Before me was a very sick man, but I wondered who Andrew was seeing in that moment. The healthy, handsome man he met decades earlier who showed so much promise? I placed a hand on Andrew's shoulder.

"Do you think he can hear us?" I whispered.

A calmness came over Andrew. I wasn't sure whether I should leave and give Andrew and Mark privacy, but it felt like Andrew didn't want to be alone. I was grateful when Father Alex arrived, a chatty priest who had known Mark for many years.

Even though I was the only one in the room who didn't know Mark, there was a strange familiarity about what was happening. I knew what it felt like to see a loved one so sick. I had been at my mother's bedside in the hospital when she died. The anticipation felt unbearable. When would death come? There was nothing you could do but wait.

Father Alex leaned closer to Mark, placing a hand on the bedsheet. "I think he might have stopped breathing," he said softly.

"Can you go get someone?" Andrew asked. I ran up the hall to the front desk and grabbed the first nurse I saw. "I think our friend just died," I said.

Back in Mark's room, the nurse held his wrist and stared at the wall, looking for a pulse. "I'm so sorry. He's gone. Is there anyone I should call for you to let them know about his passing?"

Father Alex stepped in to say a prayer. Andrew and I turned to look at each other in disbelief. Was it possible that Mark let go at that exact moment on purpose? I slid off into a corner while Andrew handled arrangements with a funeral director. Val, another friend from law school, arrived. I kept eyeing Mark's cell phone on a small table, buzzing and lighting up with messages. The last person to have touched that phone was Mark, and now he was gone. No one on the other end knew. What do you do with a cell phone after someone dies? I picked up his phone, then placed it back down.

"Betsy, right?" Father Alex said to me, a tissue in hand. "I'm so sorry for your loss. How did you know Mark?"

I didn't know how to explain the situation. To a priest, nonetheless.

"I don't. I mean, I didn't. I'm just here with Andrew. We were going to have dinner, and then, well, plans changed."

"Betsy was just supposed to ride down here with me, to keep me company," Andrew said. "We're on a date. Or at least, this was supposed to be a date."

Father Alex laughed, then stopped. "You brought a date here?" He started laughing again. "Well, how's it going?"

"Um ... pretty good, I guess," I said, glancing at Mark in the hospital bed. Was that an okay answer? The circumstances were awful, but I was still enjoying being with Andrew. How was it possible to be experiencing both at the same time?

On our way out of the room, Andrew told me to grab Mark's cell phone. It felt strange to hold such a personal thing. I hovered my finger over the off button, but that felt wrong, as if I were removing Mark's last link to the world. For everyone else in Mark's contacts list, life was still carrying on as normal. I dropped Mark's phone into the bottom of my purse.

The streets of Boston were deserted, just blinking traffic lights that we whizzed by in a blur. Every so often in the car, Mark's phone lit up. It hadn't stopped whirring and vibrating by the time we arrived at a hotel well past midnight after picking up a pizza.

"Just one night?" the receptionist asked.

Just one night. If she only knew. One night was all it took. It felt like my relationship with Andrew had been thrust ahead into another time zone, days ahead of where we were hours ago, when we left Hanover. Andrew pulled his credit card out of his wallet. He looked completely put-together in a button-down shirt, still crisp from the workday.

I couldn't believe how fast Andrew and I were moving, how unwilling I was to slow down. Our dates lasted for days on end. He showed up at my house so often that Ronan no longer barked when Andrew walked in. The two of them even figured out the perfect sleeping arrangement; Andrew curled up his legs so that Ronan would have more room to stretch out. We hung out on the couch and talked for hours, moving only to refill our coffee mugs. Many times, I wondered if I was making myself too available. I met Andrew every time he asked whether I wanted to have a drink. I texted back the second my phone dinged with a message. I said yes every time, the way I said yes when Andrew asked me to come to Boston, dropping myself even deeper into his life. I didn't know how Mark's death would change things for Andrew. He was already going through a lot.

I knew that I had been falling in love with Andrew and that I wanted to tell him at some point, but I didn't know when to do it. Mark's death ended up giving me the push I needed. One day we're here, one day we aren't, and we can't control any of it. How often the days blur together, how rarely do we appreciate being alive.

I tugged on the back of Andrew's shirt. "Andrew, I love you," I whispered. I couldn't believe I said it. Andrew turned away from the hotel counter to face me. The extra-cheese pizza in my hands blocked him from getting any closer.

"I love you too," he said.

The receptionist looked away. I couldn't wait to get him upstairs.

So now here we are in this dark hotel room, naked, our emotions laid bare and bellies full of wondrous carbohydrates, as Mark's cell phone rings on and on in the background.

"Do you think we should answer it?" Andrew asks.

"What would we say?"

The ringing stops. Andrew kisses me. How badly I wanted to play by the rules, but it turns out there's no rule book to follow, not in love, not in divorce, and certainly not when someone dies when you're on a date.

Is This a Date or a Funeral?

A woman in a slim-fitting blazer slides into the empty chair next to me at the funeral home. "I'm so sorry for your loss," she says. Mark's calling hours are wrapping up. People have been saying this to me all day, mostly hot gay men, like Mark was. Most of the seats are empty now, but there are still a few men crying, some laughing over a shared memory, passing tissues back and forth to each other.

The woman places her purse next to her chair. It looks high-end. Made of leather, probably. I once heard somewhere that Taurus people like nice purses, and now I can't help but think of that whenever I see someone with one.

"I'm Arline," she says. "Mark and I worked together in politics in Boston." Makes sense. Andrew told me that Mark was a liaison to the gay community for the mayor of Boston.

"How did you know Mark?" Arline asks.

I met him an hour before he died. I know him intimately from seeing text messages pop up on his phone, still in my purse. Probably shouldn't say either of those things. I wipe a few of Ronan's white dog hairs off my black dress. "I didn't," I say, eyeing Mark's open casket at the front of the room. Every time I see him there, I think about how short life is, that nothing is certain. Might as well be honest now. "I'm here with Andrew." We catch eyes across the room. He smiles and waves. He'd make an excellent boyfriend, the way he's comforting people, occasionally laying his hand on someone's shoulder. He has to be exhausted but doesn't look it.

"Here with Andrew?" Arline asks. "Are you a relative?"

"God, no. We're dating. We met in Hanover at a bar. He told me there was a fly in my drink. I know it sounds like a line, but there really was, and we've been hanging out ever since."

Arline turns toward me. "Isn't Andrew married?"

Oh, shit. I don't know this woman. Maybe she knows Andrew's ex. How do I answer that one? Maybe I shouldn't have come today.

I wasn't planning on it until Andrew called yesterday in need of advice. I was lying on my couch at home, snuggled under a blanket with Ronan. I put my phone on speaker. Ronan perked up at the sound of Andrew's voice.

"I need your advice," Andrew said.

Soft music was playing in the background. "Where are you?"

"I'm at JCPenney picking out a funeral suit for Mark. I don't know what color to get. Navy or black? What do you think?"

"Black seems like a safe choice."

"Black . . . okay. I'll get the black one. So, what time can I pick you up from the bus station tomorrow in Boston? The calling hours start in the late afternoon. I thought we could maybe have lunch together before—"

"The bus station? You want me to come to the funeral?" It hadn't occurred to me that I would be invited. I had only known Andrew for a month, and I didn't want to mess up our new relationship by going to a funeral where I didn't even know the person who died. Wouldn't that be like a wedding crasher but worse? Plus, Andrew's soon-to-be ex-wife might be there with Andrew's kids. "Andrew, I don't know if that's appropriate. I didn't know him."

"That doesn't matter. I'd love for you to come. Oh man, I almost forgot. I need to get Mark a tie. What do you think will be good?"

Someone in the background at JCPenney asked Andrew if he needed help. He absolutely needed help. Would he have to pick out underwear too? I imagined Andrew lost in racks of suits, overwhelmed by colorful ties. I couldn't stand the thought of him doing it alone.

"Okay, I'll come," I said.

The next morning, Andrew picked me up from the bus station in Boston. He was wearing a plaid blazer and adjusting his tie in the rearview mirror. I slid into the passenger seat in a simple black dress and knee-high boots with little tassels on the zippers. We were heading to a funeral home, but it felt like a date.

"I thought we could have lunch first," Andrew said. "I don't know about you, but I could really use a beer. There's this place called Doyle's. It's very Boston. Been around a hundred years. I think you'll like it."

I loved it. I slid my elbows onto the well-loved bar and took in all the history: campaign posters for John F. Kennedy, creaky wooden booths with red-and-white checkered tablecloths, photos of Boston policemen, scuffed-up hardwood floors.

"So, good news," Andrew said. "My ex isn't coming to the funeral tomorrow . . ."

I popped a French fry in my mouth. "Great!"

"But my mother is."

I reached for Andrew's water glass. "You're joking."

"Don't worry. She's easy. You can call her Kitty, short for Katherine." Andrew slid an arm around the back of my barstool. "You look wonderful today. Have I told you that yet?" He hadn't, but my bangs were behaving, and I managed to get my eyeliner in a straight line.

Now, back at the funeral home, Arline checks the time on her phone, then leans back in her chair. "You know, I have to tell you. For losing one of his best friends and going through a divorce, Andrew looks good. He seems happy, like a totally different person. I haven't seen him like this in a while."

That feels nice to hear. Susan said the same thing about me the other night. Love does more for your appearance than Botox. "You'd never guess that he's having some pretty big astrological transits right now," I say.

Arline laughs. "I love astrology! What's your sign? I'm a Taurus."

It always feels good to find someone who is into astrology, like you're speaking a secret language. "I had a feeling," I say. "Your purse was a giveaway."

She laughs, then turns her attention back to Mark. "Do you know what cemetery he's being buried at?"

"They're going to cremate him and have a ceremony to spread his ashes next summer in Provincetown. Mark and Andrew went there all the time. Andrew's dad had a house on the beach. Lots of history there."

Maybe I'll be invited to that too. I imagine Andrew and I on the Cape six months from now, strolling up and down the shores in summertime, seals bobbing their heads out of the water. I'd give anything for a salty ocean breeze, margaritas on the rocks, tank tops, sundresses. How is it that I barely had the guts to show up today, but I'm already dreaming up a future with Andrew six months from now?

"It's so sad what happened to Mark," Arlene says. "So young, so talented. I always hoped AA would work for him. I know he went to a couple different rehab centers. He was sick for years . . ."

It's a sad story, and I wish that Mark hadn't suffered so terribly at the hands of his addiction. And yet, how odd that his death has set my life in motion. If Mark hadn't died, I wouldn't be here right now at a Boston funeral home witnessing how great Andrew is during a tragedy. I wouldn't be meeting Kitty tomorrow at the funeral. I wouldn't have spent the better part of today drinking wine, kissing, and eating grilled cheese—three of my favorite things. I'd probably be at home on Susan's couch, watching my phone, waiting for life to happen to me, for Andrew to text. That's the upside of death; it forces you to live in the moment.

Arline leans in closer. "So, if you don't mind me asking, how's your date going so far?"

Funny, Father Alex asked me the same thing. In moments of darkness, we all yearn for signs of love. I wave at Andrew across the room. Thank God I got on the bus this morning. "Really good, actually."

Did You Get the Email?

I pry open Susan's old, boxy cooler. It looks like it could be used to transport organs, except it contains the cocktails that she made before we left the house.

We're packed into Susan's car on a blustery fall evening drinking her homemade Manhattans to save a few bucks by pregaming dinner.

Susan spins around from the driver's seat. "So, how was the funeral? Did you meet Andrew's mom? What did you wear?"

"Here's all you need to know," Andrew says. "She stood up in front of everyone and read the petitions at the funeral home, just like a good Catholic girl."

I twist open the thermos. "The priest asked me to! You should have never told him I went to Catholic school. He asked me if I had ever considered coming back to the church. They'd never take me if they knew the truth, that a married man sleeps in my bed every night."

Susan eyes Andrew in the rearview mirror. "Andrew, how is your divorce going? What's the latest?"

I think Susan secretly wishes she were still a divorce lawyer so that she could represent Andrew. She thinks she can solve his problems, and Andrew likes the arrangement because he gets a therapist for free.

"Oh man, you're never going to believe what happened to me," Andrew says. "You might want to put your cup down for this so you don't spill. My ex sent every high school football player and their parents an email with the financial details of our divorce . . ."

Jake erupts in laughter. "You gotta be shitting me! That's worse than anything that ever happened in my divorce, and my divorce was *bad*."

"Was it an accident? It had to be," I say.

Andrew sips his drink, then winces. "You wouldn't believe what was in there. Our bank account information ... credit card debt ..."

"What was the subject line?" I ask. "Maybe not everyone opened it?" Of course everyone opened it. What am I saying? I would open it.

"This will be the talk of the town at the awards banquet," Andrew says.

"Isn't your son on the football team?" Susan asks.

"He's the quarterback."

I imagine Andrew's son opening the email in the locker room, on the practice field, in the cafeteria. His friends asking him, "Did you get the email?" How on Earth would he explain that? I would be mortified. I have never met him, and I am mortified for him. Divorce is truly awful. Maybe it was for the best that Jack and I didn't have kids. Ronan didn't have to explain anything to anyone.

"Who was she trying to send the email to?" Jake asks.

"Does it matter? It went to every person on the Friends of Hanover Football email list, including me. And she knew! And didn't tell me."

I always felt like my divorce was sad because Jack and I didn't have much to divide between us, but maybe that wasn't so bad. Maybe it's worse when it's the other way around.

"Sounds like you need a refill, Andrew," Susan says. "Hand me your glass."

"Can we go inside soon?" I ask. "I'm getting hungry." From my seat in the car, I can see little lights dangling from the ceiling inside Burdick's restaurant, and a chalkboard with hand-scribbled specials. I imagine all four of us cozy inside, angling for another piece of bread, menus splattered with red wine stains. Susan will probably ask the waiter for extra butter.

Andrew leans over to kiss my earlobe. "Will you be my appetizer tonight?"

"I was planning to be your dessert!" A splash of my drink lands on Susan's back seat.

"Don't spill any of that!" Susan yells. "We're low on rations, and I'm sick of my car smelling like a bar. No sex in the back seat either!"

"But *we* can still do it back there, right, honey?" Jake asks, tapping a gloved hand on Susan's leg.

Burdick's is the latest spot where the four of us have double-dated. The other night, we caught a movie at the Nugget Theater and went to Pine for cocktails. Sometimes, we play board games, though it can get pretty competitive. I'm doubling down on Andrew with every day that passes. I don't want a thing to change, though there are plenty of reminders that Andrew is in transition, like the time he asked Susan and Jake if he should buy a used Land Rover, or when he left the house without his glasses, which felt like a weird metaphor. Maybe he wasn't seeing clearly.

I was sure he was flat-out crazy when he suggested we have professional photos taken of us on a getaway to Provincetown a couple weekends ago. We wandered down Commercial Street on a Saturday afternoon, but most of the shops were closed because it was November, except for one, a photography studio.

"Let's have our photos taken!" Andrew said.

I thought he had lost his mind. What was there to commemorate? We hadn't been together long. "Don't you think that's kind of weird?"

"It'll be fun! Anything goes in P-town. I'm sure Brad has photographed plenty of naked men during Bear Week. We're nothing compared to what he's seen."

Even though Andrew and I spend plenty of time talking about the future, doubt creeps in all the time. I worry that my happiness could disappear, like it did in my marriage. That day, I couldn't shake the feeling that the photo session would jinx my good fortune. I didn't even have anything special to wear. I showed up in my plain black winter coat and the furry boots I bought with Susan at Farm-Way.

"Andrew, take Betsy's hand, and walk toward me," Brad said, clicking away on the beach.

I could barely see Andrew. My hair was flying in every direction. We tried to gain our footing as our boots sank into the sand. I was grateful that it was the off-season, that we were alone at the beach.

"So, what's the occasion for your photos?" Brad asked.

"We just started dating!" Andrew said.

I winced. Brad took a few more pictures. It sounded so ridiculous. Just dating. Not a birthday or an anniversary. And Brad didn't even know the whole story, that Andrew was still technically married to someone else and interviewing for jobs in other cities. Our relationship was as messy as a beach photo shoot. What if Andrew and I broke up? What would I do with the photos then?

"New relationship! Love it!" Brad yelled back.

I had expected our photos to be terrible, but there ended up being so many good ones that it was hard to choose. We looked happy. My insecurity was visible only to me. I had been so sure it wasn't the right time to have our photo taken, but it never occurred to me that there might be beauty in the mess. I love seeing the photos on the wall in my apartment now when I walk through the door.

Susan spins around again from the driver's seat. "What was Andrew's mother like?"

"She told me to call her 'Kitty.' Do you think that means she likes me?"

"Obviously she likes you. Maybe you just met your future mother-in-law!"

Marriage? With Andrew? Could I do that again?

I don't want to end up sending out the details of my divorce to the football team, but I sure do like thinking about our beach photos hanging on the wall of our own home one day. I never, ever thought I'd say this, but maybe I could get married again, despite the ugliness of divorce. Maybe it's not Andrew who's crazy. Maybe it's me.

Cobwebs and Dust Bunnies

Andrew and I didn't make it up in time for *Jeopardy!* tonight, not that I was in the mood anyway.

"I'm coming over with your drinks—watch the dogs," Susan says, placing them on the Formica coffee table in front of us. She clicks on a lamp, then plops herself down into her favorite red leather chair.

"Shit, Jake, I forgot about *our* drinks. I was too worried about the kids."

By the kids, she means me and Andrew. Jake shuffles across the room to get them.

"So, how are you two lovebirds doing?" Susan asks.

No one wants Susan's sarcasm tonight. No one lifts a glass. There's nothing to toast. The day I worried about for several months is finally here. Andrew has been offered a job in Greenville, South Carolina, and has taken it.

I sip my drink. "Do you have a leaving date yet?"

Andrew shakes his head. "Not yet."

Am I supposed to say congratulations? It's winter. How am I going to make it to spring without him? What I need is more time with Andrew.

Andrew places his drink on the windowsill behind us. "I'll take the job in Greenville, and I'll come back to visit you in Hanover every other weekend."

Long distance, the kiss of death. Can I do that? I don't know. It's a good job opportunity for Andrew, but that doesn't make it any easier. I know I don't *want* to do long distance. "Susan, can you make me another drink?"

"You haven't finished the one you have," she replies.

"I will finish this one in three more sips. Might as well make another one for Andrew since he's going to leave me for a Southern woman."

"No one will compare to you," he says.

"Then why are you going?"

"I've been here for a decade. It's time for something new."

I can't argue with him; I did the same thing. After eleven years in New York and a divorce, I skipped town too. Andrew's been honest this whole time. How can I be angry? But what about Ronan? They were just starting to get close to each other, and now he'll have no father figure.

Jake mutes the television, takes a hit off his vape, then passes it to Susan. "I think we're going to need this tonight."

Even the dogs sense trouble is on the horizon. Usually, they're on the couch with us, begging for attention, but they're far away now, curled up on the rug, not within arm's reach of a snuggle. Maybe they sense that soon there will be room on the couch next to me when Andrew's gone for good. Are they just biding their time, the way I was while waiting for Andrew to tell me he was leaving but secretly hoping all along he'd stay?

"I have an idea," I say. "Ask Siri if you should move to Greenville. She always has the answers for you."

I never knew anyone who used the iPhone's virtual assistant before I met Andrew, let alone someone who programmed his Siri to talk like an Australian woman. There isn't anything he doesn't ask her about. When Andrew and I started dating, he used her to ask when C&A Pizza closed, what the weather forecast was, and how old Paul Rudd was. We always loved to guess the ages of celebrities. Guess we won't be doing that anymore.

"Hey, Siri, should I move to Greenville?" Andrew asks.

"I don't know what you mean," Siri replies.

Neither do I. How can Andrew and I possibly go from spending every night together to seeing each other every other weekend? A few weeks ago, Andrew told me he loved me. Now this. "I wonder if this is because Saturn is in your first house right now."

Susan winces. "You're fucked. Saturn is the planet that always screws everyone over."

Do I really want Susan and Jake witnessing this spat I'm having with Andrew? I guess I do. This actually feels like a family meeting. My entire relationship with Andrew has played out in front of Susan and Jake in the living room, so why should this time be different?

"I get wanting to leave Hanover . . ." I say. "I couldn't wait to leave New York after my divorce, but why do you have to leave right this second?"

Andrew sips his drink, then places it on the coffee table. "I can't handle it anymore. This town is too small. I don't want to keep running into people from my old life. I nearly hit my ex-wife with my car by accident crossing Main Street today." He swigs the last dribble from his glass. "Come with me. Let's get out of here."

Should I go with him? Is Andrew my exit strategy? For an entire year, I've been wondering where I'll go next. Here's my chance. Except, now that I have the chance, I don't want to go anywhere. "I can't. I'm happy here."

I can't imagine South Carolina would be better than the life I have here now. I would miss the seasons, and I would miss my life with Susan and Jake. I've just hit a rhythm with my work. I can't agree to something I know is wrong in my heart.

"Why can't you just stay a while longer? This idea of leaving right now is the dumbest idea you've ever had!"

Jake dumps another log on the fire. "Betsy, don't take this the wrong way, but you sound a lot like my wife tonight."

Andrew is on his phone, swiping through photos of homes to rent. "Maybe I'll find something good and entice you to come with me."

As much as the running of the dogs has ruined any decent sleep I'll ever get, I can't imagine waking up in any other house. This is terrible. I am losing Andrew in December, the dead of winter, the worst possible time of year. A frozen driveway is just around the corner. I imagine myself in my bed, alone, snow falling outside my bedroom window, Ronan's big head warming my legs. A clump of dust clinging to a corner of the living room ceiling catches my eye. That's all I'll notice after Andrew leaves. I'll have nothing left to do but stare off into space at cobwebs and dust bunnies.

"I started looking for jobs *before* I met you," Andrew says. "Our timing is terrible."

"Not true!" I think back to the first time we met, at Pine, when two empty seats opened up. That was certainly good timing. What if the fly hadn't flown into my drink? Would Andrew even have talked to me? And Mark's death in the hospital when Andrew and I were both in the room. Dreadful, but it brought us closer together.

Jake leans over from his chair to take Susan's hand. "Gosh, I don't think I've ever been happier to be married to you."

"How many times did you guys get together and break up before you got married?" Andrew asks.

"Too many!" Susan says. "Don't forget that Jake was going through a divorce when I met him too!"

"Was he?" I know they used to be neighbors in Montpelier, but that's it.

"I walked her dog when she was at work," Jake says. "Then her old boyfriend stole her dog, and I went and got it back for her!"

"You guys are together because of a dog?" I can't think of a better meet-cute than that.

"We also had a few bumps in the road . . ." Jake says.

"He went to Florida with this other woman, and I retaliated. I got really skinny, and I had men crawling everywhere. I was the 'it girl' in Montpelier!"

I wouldn't mind being the "it girl" of Hanover, but I don't want to be on-and-off like Susan and Jake were. I just want to have a normal relationship. On all the time. That's all I want. Why can't Andrew just sit tight for a little while longer?

Susan hasn't intervened much tonight. It's so unlike her. Maybe she's been so quiet because she's been here herself. She's been quiet because she knows what I've been too scared to admit. She already knows our breakup is coming.

Andrew pops the maraschino cherry from his empty glass into his mouth, but he still has the one I gave him. I never eat the cherry. "Well,

I want to be with someone who would follow me to Greenville. If the situation were reversed, I'd tell you to take the job, and I'd follow you there. It's a great opportunity for me. Why can't you be happy for me?"

I'm not happy for Andrew. Maybe that makes me a bad person, but I can't help it. I don't want him to go, but I'm not going to convince him to stay. The one thing I don't want to do is hang on too tight like I did in my marriage. As hard as it is to let Andrew go, if it's something he wants, then he should have that.

Andrew slides the last maraschino cherry down his toothpick and into his mouth. "You don't want to be here anyway. Do you even realize how much you complain about Hanover? It's too small . . . there's no good bars . . . there's no good pizza . . . you fell on the icy driveway six times. Do you know how many times you tell that story about the bartender in Vermont making you a margarita with vodka instead of tequila?"

He's right. I know I tell that story a lot, but it's a good one, and as much as I complain about this town, I actually love it here. I can't believe that moving to Ronan's hometown actually worked out for me, well until now, at least. "I can't follow you. It's only been three months. I don't want to do long distance. I know myself. I'm not good with it."

Andrew's phone dings with a congratulatory text from a friend. He smiles big and taps out a response. I feel like I've just collapsed onto a deflating air mattress. "I wish I had never met you!" I yell.

Andrew drops his phone onto the couch, stunned. "You don't mean that."

I don't, but I know that I'd be winning more at *Jeopardy!* and have read more books. Is there a point to opening up your heart if it all ends this way? I *want* to be mad so that it's easier to let him go. But really, I just want him here with me always.

"Let's try long distance," Andrew says.

I lift my iPhone to my lips. "Hey, Siri, how far is Greenville from here?"

Until I met Andrew, I never used Siri. I always considered myself an old-fashioned texter, but when I saw how easy Siri was, Andrew had me using it in no time at all, especially when I realized that I could program

Siri to speak with a male Irish accent. On our lazy weekend mornings, I asked Siri what movies were playing at the Nugget. I had her pull up menus from Tuk Tuk, our favorite Thai restaurant for takeout. Now, I'm asking Siri to plan a life without Andrew.

"Greenville is located 984 miles away," Siri says.

Too far. There's no point. It already feels like Andrew and I are the furthest apart we've ever been.

One Empty Barstool

Susan pulls out a barstool, then pours coffee into my mug. "Sit. Jake is making the three of us breakfast." There are four barstools gathered around the breakfast bar, like usual, but one of them is empty: Andrew's. We all used to sit here together and jostle for the last bite of one of Susan's pasta dishes. Andrew and I played footsies in our wool socks, and Rooney sat in between us, hoping for scraps.

Susan pulls a carton of eggs and homemade sourdough bread out from the fridge. "Let's talk about what happened with you and Andrew last night."

I bury my head in my hands. What a stupid idea to have more than one cocktail. I'm heartbroken and hungover, a terrible combination. "There's nothing to talk about. We're done." I wrap my favorite wool cardigan around my T-shirt so Jake and Susan can't see that I haven't even bothered to put on a bra this morning. "I know what you're trying to do by attempting to feed me, and it isn't going to work. I'm not hungry, and my train leaves soon, the one I told you about. Amtrak to New York City. Train 55, the *Vermonter*."

I need to get out of Hanover as soon as possible. An hour ago, I got off the phone with Andrew. I told him that I couldn't do long distance, that I didn't want to spend the next month watching him pack up and start a new life without me. I felt bad calling him at work, but I was desperate to feel like I had control of the situation. I had hoped that maybe he'd object, but all he said was that he understood my decision.

"So, you haven't heard from Andrew at all?" Susan asks.

"Not since you called him this morning." Earlier when I was in the laundry room, I heard Susan upstairs on the telephone. "Women say things they don't mean all the time ... she booked a train to New York ... you need to come and stop her ..."

I set the laundry basket on the floor, then crept up the stairs, trying to not disturb the dogs when I arrived on the landing in the living room. Susan was in her chair, landline pressed to her ear, gazing out the window at the few remaining leaves swirling around in the wind. She nearly dropped the phone when she saw me. "Okay, Joe. I gotta go now, bye-bye."

"I'm not dumb!" I yelled. "I know that wasn't your son. Was that Andrew?"

"Betsy, you don't understand. Men need to be told what to do. Come here, sit down on the couch. Let's talk this through."

"There's nothing left to decide. He's made his choice! Stay off the phone! Mind your own business! Who still has a landline anyway?" I yelled.

Now, as Susan and Jake putter around the kitchen, I wonder if Susan was convincing enough to get Andrew to come over, but I guess it won't matter. I'm leaving soon.

Jake slides a piece of buttered toast onto my plate. "There's more coming."

"Just admit it. You called Andrew. I can't believe you did that."

Susan takes another sip of coffee.

"Well?" I ask.

Jake spins around from the stove to face us. Spatula in hand, he nudges Susan. "You told me you did."

"Jesus, Jake," Susan says. "Work with me here. And turn up the heat on those eggs."

My heart feels more broken than the cracked eggshells that Jake's left on the counter. Why can't I just have a normal relationship? A marriage that lasts more than several years and a boyfriend who lasts more than three months? "I don't have time to eat." I stand and push my barstool back in. "My train leaves in an hour."

Susan and Jake eye each other. "Sit," Susan says. "You haven't finished your eggs and toast."

"I'm not hungry."

"Come on, Betsy," Jake says. "I made them for you."

I can't argue with Jake. He looks so sweet in his apron spooning fluffy eggs out onto my plate from the skillet. I take one bite, then stop. I'm not hungry. Maybe I'll stop having an appetite, and then I can lose all the weight I've put on dating Andrew.

I pull out the barstool and rest my elbows on the counter. I sat here after I couldn't get a car, after my bad job interview, after I found Jack's wedding ring. I ate Susan's cookies on Christmas when I was missing my mother, toasted my glass to celebrate Ronan's puppies. There is something about this counter that grounds me. I hope that my situation with Andrew will all work out, though I can't imagine how.

"Why did you break up with Andrew?" Susan asks, folding her hands.

"It was a test, to see what he would do. You know, put the ball in his corner. He didn't object."

"A test?? No!! Men don't need tests. They need to be trained like dogs. They don't understand anything, at least not in the beginning."

Jake offers me another warm slice of bread. "That's right. I'm in my seventies, and I still don't know what I'm doing."

That doesn't give me a lot of confidence. Rooney brushes past my legs. I drop a piece of crust for her. Susan lets it slide. I eye the clock in Susan's kitchen, the same one I glanced at when Andrew and I spent late nights in Susan's living room, unable to believe we had all been hanging out for as many hours as we had, but that's over now. I have less than an hour to get to the train station. I can't imagine staying here after Andrew leaves town, showing up at all the places he and I liked to go. Pine for cocktails, Cedar Circle for coffee, Trail Break for burritos. There will always be an empty seat beside me.

Jake pours coffee into his mug, then mine. "Betsy, I have to tell you something."

"You mixed bacon grease with the eggs?"

"I texted Andrew too."

"You did what?!"

"It's okay, don't worry. I told him that he was making a mistake and needed to think about what he was doing. That's what went wrong in my first marriage, I worked too much. All work, no time for family."

"Drove me nuts," Susan says.

"Look at the two of you, trying to keep Andrew from leaving. I can't believe any of this. You're supposed to be loyal to *me*."

"Do you think he'll come back to get his stuff when you're gone?" Susan asks.

Ugh. I haven't even thought of that. Now, I'm going to have to deal with all the clothes and furniture Andrew moved in here the last three months. "What should I do with Andrew's painting in the garage? The weird one of the woman, the one that you always thought was his ex-wife?"

Jake slams his fists down on the counter. "Let's burn it!"

"Better yet—let's have a yard sale!" Susan says. "Let's move all of his things out into the front yard and make some money off of your ex-boyfriend!"

My ex-boyfriend. I hate the sound of that.

Susan sips her coffee. "Do you want me to call him again?"

"NO!" I yell, waking Rooney from her nap on the rug. "Neither of you will message him! You've already done enough. If you do, I promise you that I will take an Uber to the train station." This is an empty threat. We all know it's as hard to get a taxi in Hanover as it is to start my old car in below-zero temperatures.

"I know you booked a train ticket, but I think leaving now is a terrible idea," Susan says. "I think you should stay."

I have to admit I am as tired of running as I am of Susan nagging me about it. I left home after my mother died. I left New York after I got divorced. And now I'm taking off again.

"Do you love Andrew?" Susan asks.

"Susan! You can't ask her that," Jake says.

"Yes, I can. I am her mother figure. I need to know."

I wish I didn't love Andrew right now, but I can't help it. "I do, even though he's leaving me."

"Can't you try and make it work?"

I don't know what else I could do. Maybe I could try visiting Greenville with him, just to rule it out completely. I don't think I'll want to live there, but I could at least try. I've tried to get closure by breaking up, but I'm still confused. "The waiting feels too unbearable."

"Stay. If you do, I'll make something good for dinner tonight."

She knows how to bargain with me. But what will I do the rest of the day? At some point, I'll have to go back downstairs to my life and sit with the sadness. Even if I'm on that train to New York, all my memories of Andrew will be right next to me in the passenger seat. All I can do is wait until the feeling passes. At least I know how to be alone now.

"I'll help you deal with Andrew's stuff," Susan says. "We could have a fire sale!"

I indulge myself with the thought of Andrew coming back to the house today and finding his stuff outside in the gravel driveway, with local Hanover residents pawing through all his things. I imagine Susan haggling with someone over the price of Andrew's Peloton bike, a fat wad of $20 bills in her pocket, trying to get a better deal for me, and Jake holding up a pair of Andrew's work pants to see if he might be able to wear them himself. Andrew has already given Jake a few old suits. I hope I never see them on Jake. I love how much Susan and Jake want to take down Andrew, although I don't really want them to do that because I still love Andrew. And I know they love him too.

The Butterfly Effect

Someone's knocking on my apartment door. That rarely happens. Ronan barks, then dashes to the door so fast that he manages to knock a magnet off my refrigerator. I hold my breath, hoping it's Andrew, but I know it won't be. We just had another argument about our future.

"Betsy, it's me," Susan says. "Can I come in?"

Ugh. I collapse onto the couch and cover myself with a warm wool blanket I bought in Ireland. I accidentally put it in the dryer, so now it's too small. I can't think of the last time Susan has come downstairs to my apartment, but Ronan is thrilled to see her. He balances up on his hind legs, and his tongue rolls out of his mouth and drips a little bit of drool onto my hardwood floors.

"Down, Ronan!" Susan says. "Where are his manners?"

She doesn't mean it. She rubs the sides of Ronan's head, right by his ears; he moans in delight.

My coffee table is cluttered with stacks of grease-stained magazines and crinkled newspapers, the morning's dirty dishes still piled up in the sink. I feel a twinge of guilt, like I've disappointed my parents or something. I would have tidied up if I knew she was coming downstairs. Ronan paws at Susan's legs for attention, balancing his white furry paws up on the armrest. "Why don't you brush him more? Look at all these tangles . . ."

"Stop criticizing me." This is the last thing I need right now, someone telling me what I'm doing wrong. "I'm not in the mood."

Susan grabs Ronan's palm brush from a nearby table and tries to detangle the fur under his arms. She gazes out the window. "Looks dreary out there, doesn't it? At least it doesn't snow in Greenville."

Andrew and I just got back from a long weekend in South Carolina to see if we could start over there together, but I couldn't see myself living there. I would miss the seasons, even winter. Outside my living room window, the tall, thin pines are swaying back and forth. The garden beds are nothing now but piles of mud and dirt, with a few dead tendrils from my tomato plant clinging to the dog fence. All my taxi tomatoes are gone, so are the lavender plants and the French tarragon that Susan said would be life-changing. Any day now, a foot of snow will be on the ground.

"How's it going with Andrew? Is he staying or going?"

"Going, as of this morning."

Ronan runs to the back door, then presses his nose against the floor, sniffing. His tail swishes back and forth double-time. The doorknob turns. It's Andrew.

"I was trying to stall, so you wouldn't leave," Susan says.

"You knew about this?"

Andrew hasn't bothered taking off his winter boots. There's slush all over the hardwood floors. More mess for me to clean up when he and Susan leave. He sits down next to me on the couch and takes off his glasses, foggy from the heat.

"It took you forever to get here," Susan says.

"You knew he was coming and didn't tell me?" I ask.

Another knock at the door. Ronan barks. "Who's left?"

Susan sighs. "Probably my deadbeat husband."

"Hey, Betsy. Are you in there? Did you hear from Andrew? I thought I saw his car just pull into the driveway. Can I come in to check out the furnace? If you're naked, I can give you a minute."

Susan rolls her eyes. "Jesus Christ, Jake. Come in!"

Jake opens the door. "Oh, wow—the gang's all here." He sits down in the only available chair, resting an elbow on my flowered tablecloth, scattered with papers from the freelance work I was trying to do before everyone showed up, though all I was doing was reading the same sentence over again. "So, what's the latest? Andrew, you're not really going to skip town, are you? Don't break up the party."

I'd love to know what Andrew's plans are. Is he here to pick up that weird painting that's been sitting in the garage for months? Or is he here to tell me he's going to stay, then change his mind tomorrow ...

"Jake, I think our work here is done," Susan says. "If anyone needs CBD or something stronger, you know where to find me."

"It's not even noon," Andrew says.

"That means it's happy hour in Ireland. Come on, Jake." She shuts the door behind them.

Ronan jumps onto the couch, then places his head on Andrew's lap. Ronan will be devastated when Andrew leaves. "Shouldn't you be at work giving your notice?"

"I was going to, but now I don't know. I was really hoping you would come to Greenville with me. I know I've been indecisive, but this has been hard."

I know he's sorry, but it feels like our relationship is on pause. When I started dating, I knew the chances of meeting someone who had been married were pretty good, but I hadn't counted on meeting someone who wasn't even divorced yet. I push the blanket off my legs. "Andrew, I can't do this anymore. One day you're here, one day you're leaving. One day you tell me you love me, one day you're out the door before I even wake up." Ronan crawls onto my lap. "I get it. I'm divorced too. I know more than anyone how hard it is to start over, but I can't handle the uncertainty."

"Hang on, I have something to say." Ronan tilts his big head at Andrew, then at me. "Well, okay. What I want to say is that I've been married for twenty-five years. I don't know what I'm doing, but I know I love you."

I always thought love was enough, but maybe it's not. Life is too complicated. What makes a relationship actually work? I have no idea.

"I love you too, but I can't handle the ups and downs anymore."

Ronan shifts back onto Andrew's lap. "I don't want to move unless you're coming with me."

"I'm not moving," I say. "I'm happy here. Why do you have to leave right now? Can't you just stick around a little while longer? For Ronan's sake. Look how much he loves you. He needs a man in his life."

Andrew laughs. "Funny you should say that. I have to tell you what happened to me this morning." Andrew takes his phone out of his pocket. "I was getting off the highway and pulled up right behind this car. Check out the license plate!"

I peer over Andrew's shoulder as he flips through his iPhone photos. There's a few of us in Boston, a couple of us here in my apartment with Ronan. He stops on a photo of an SUV with Massachusetts license plates. "Are you kidding me?"

Andrew can't stop laughing. "I couldn't believe it either."

There's only one word on the license plate, but those five letters make all the difference in the world right now.

RONAN

Ronan. The name Jack and I chose for our new dog five years ago. Never in my wildest dreams did I think it would have such a huge effect now, years later. I imagine Andrew cruising along, listening to Vermont Public Radio, seeing the license plate, scrambling to find his phone so that he could hurry up and take a picture. I'm glad he took a photo because this is so wild, I wouldn't have ever believed him. If that driver in front of Andrew only knew what was on the line when he got in his car this morning and turned on the ignition.

"Did you flag him down?" I ask. "I would have put my flashers on and jumped out of the car."

If Jack and I had chosen the name Jimmy or Seamus, like I had initially wanted, would Andrew even be here with me right now? What if we hadn't seen that valet ticket in the parking garage? I think about that every time I drive past the hotel in Hanover where we found the ticket.

Andrew takes my hand. "It felt like a sign seeing that license plate."

I agree. It feels too meaningful to be a coincidence, and it's enough to make me want to try one more time with Andrew. I zoom in on the license plate with my fingers. Now I see why the name Ronan felt right to me all those years ago. It contained my entire future.

A Big Life in a Small Town

I zip up my coat, yank my wool beanie over my head, and open the bathroom door. "Andrew, I'm leaving!"

He peeks out from behind the shower curtain. "I love you. Don't forget to write me into your future!"

I kiss his wet face. I absolutely want Andrew in my future, but what does that mean? Will we get married? Have children? How long will we live in Susan's house? Maybe today, I'll find the answers.

Susan and I are driving to a new coffee shop in Vermont named for the First Branch of the White River, close to where Bridget, Annie, and I went tubing in the summer. We're planning to do a writing exercise that she learned from her son called "The ten-year plan for a remarkable life," where you're supposed to write down what you want your life to look like a decade from now.

I toss Ronan a dog biscuit on my way out the door. He wags his tail, then jumps back up onto the couch in his favorite spot. Maybe I'll write puppies into his future.

By the time I arrive in the driveway, Susan has flipped on my car seat warmer. I don't have heated seats in my Toyota Corolla, but my car is still running, and that's good enough for me.

We cross the Connecticut River, then head north through rolling hills. The scene unfolds like a wintry Christmas card, with a dusting of snow on the pines and a cleared path for the occasional ski trail. We pull off a deserted highway exit and turn onto a quiet back road dotted with old churches and a one-room post office.

The coffee shop reminds me of a New York City art gallery, open and airy with large windows casting sunlight onto old, dusty hardwood floors. The coffee grinder whirs. There's a small nook at the front entrance with two seats that overlook a village green and a snow-covered gazebo. "Grab those," I say.

I return with two frothy espresso drinks, a cream-filled chocolate donut, and a warm cheddar biscuit sliced in two. Small ice crystals are forming around the window. Susan has already pulled out her computer. I brought a notebook and my journal that has a full moon and pine trees on the cover. "So, have you thought about your plan yet?"

Susan slips off her coat and pops a bite of biscuit into her mouth. In a decade, Susan will be in her seventies, and Jake will be in his eighties. I will be forty-eight. It's weird to think of where I might be ten years on.

A few customers saunter in, dragging sloppy puddles over the floor in their heavy winter boots.

"I'm not sure where to start," I say, flipping my notebook to a blank page. It's the same feeling I had when I knew my marriage wasn't going to work, overwhelmed and unsure what to do next.

"Just start at the beginning, when the day begins."

Okay. Easy enough.

I wake up naturally, with no alarm clock. My husband tells me good morning.

Married! Wow, I really surprised myself with that one.

What about Ronan? I know that he won't live forever, but I'd like him to live as long as reasonably possible. I'd also like one of his puppies. Maybe we could do another sex party in Susan's backyard. Ronan could still be alive a decade from now. A slim chance is all I need.

Ronan is still alive (even though he's 15), and today he's doing well because he had acupuncture yesterday.

I don't think I could handle five dogs like Susan and Jake, but I'll take three.

We live in a small town—there are lots of trees. I can see them out the bedroom window. There's also lots of sun. I love my house.

Susan is still next to me typing like a crazy woman.

"Are you asking for the moon and the stars over there or something?" I ask?

"I'm still in bed," she says, her mouth full of donut. "I have a Marimekko bedspread and linen sheets!"

"Guess what? I'm getting married!"

I've been thinking of Andrew as I describe the relationship I have with my husband, who's funny and talkative and likes to travel, but something is stopping me from writing down his name. I realize that even now, in this imaginary exercise, I'm still scared to fail. I worry about finding this notebook a decade from now, the future me looking back at the past me with the benefit of hindsight, unable to believe how I could have been so wrong about everything. It's how I feel when I come across my wedding album.

"I could do your wedding," Susan says. "I used to marry people when I was a justice of the peace. What else does your future hold?"

I want to write creatively, for myself, for the rest of my life. I want to believe that I can make a living this way, that the work that feeds my soul can pay a mortgage. I have never written a word of fiction in my life, but in the future, I write a novel that takes place in Ireland. I travel around the world to do readings at independent bookstores. I had been thinking about joining a writing group. Maybe I should look into that. I turn the page ...

I have a book reading in town. No time to bike to the bookstore—I'll have to take the convertible! I pull my hair into a ponytail and look at myself in the rearview mirror. No grays—whew! I can't believe I'm turning fifty in two years, but I'm happy, and that's all that matters.

Do what makes you happy, as my mother said. I've realized it's the small things that bring me the most pleasure, the view of the Connecticut River when I cross the bridge from New Hampshire into Vermont. Growing my own tomatoes and taking long bike rides to the farm where Andrew and I had our first kiss. Playing *Jeopardy!* and walking Ronan with Andrew.

Susan has abandoned her fad diets for yoga. She's living in a home that my husband helped design and has a dog named Moxie, a puppy from Rooney.

"Is Rooney still alive?" I ask.

Susan shakes her head.

"What happened to her?"

"It doesn't matter. She lived a good life. All those puppies she brought into the world! She was a great mother..."

"She *is* a great mother. She's still alive, remember?"

Susan says she lives somewhere warm with a view of the sea out her bedroom window. "It's what Jake's always wanted. You know how much he hates being cold. He wants us to move to Florida."

I can't imagine myself living in Florida. I would miss the seasons. We stare at each other, stumped. I hadn't considered this. How will our futures align? If Susan is living at the beach, and I'm living in the woods, how will that work? I want to be close enough that we can all have dinner together, like we do now.

"There are places where you can have trees and the ocean," Susan says. "Like the Carolinas! I'd love to live there."

I'm not sure where we will end up, but I know Susan and I will stay in each other's lives. I'll need her help if I ever have kids. Oh man, what am I going to do about that? That question has caused me so much anxiety in my life. I turn another page...

I wasn't sure if I wanted children, but something happened that made it clear.

I don't know what that something is, but I'm trying to leave a little room for life to do its magical thing and surprise me. Will it be a young woman who walks through the door of this coffee shop with a newborn in a stroller? Will it be a serious conversation that Andrew and I have tonight about children? What I want is for something good to come from those four eggs I froze. How funny that I wasn't even sure I'd end up using them, but now it's feeling more like a possibility as I read aloud.

My daughter was a miracle baby. She came out of the four eggs I froze. I always worried about having children, but I am 48 now, and I don't live my life with fear anymore.

"Guess what? I have you having two children," she says.

"You do?"

"I babysit, and Jake teaches them how to recycle."

I spoon out the milky foam from the bottom of my cappuccino, then place my teacup back onto the table. "I think I'd be lucky to have one child. But two. How would that be possible?"

There I go again, tripping myself up. Thinking about the mechanics of everything when I should just say what I want and let life find a way.

Susan loops her scarf around her neck. "Are you writing about Andrew? In your future? Is he the one you end up with?"

I hope so, but our relationship is still new. He's not even divorced yet, and I know by now that love isn't a sure thing. It's impossible to know whether we'll marry one day, but he is the one I've been thinking of this entire time. "I want a future with Andrew." There. I said it aloud. And I can't take it back.

"He could end up being your husband! He gave up those jobs in California and South Carolina for you. That's love."

Maybe we will end up together. Who knows what will happen? I've felt like I was running out of time ever since I got divorced, but now after doing this writing exercise, maybe I have more time than I thought.

A few more customers shuffle in; a gust of cold air sneaks in behind them. Winter is here, but something tells me the season will be a lot more enjoyable than last year. Funny to think that of all the other cities or countries I could be living in ten years on, the only place I want to be is where I already am.

"Come on, let's keep going," Susan says. Within seconds, her fingers are clicking on her keyboard. I open my journal to where I left off and pick up my pen. My future is just about to begin.

One Less Puppy Person to Screen

It's just before midnight when I arrive at the vet's office and find Susan in a corner of the room. "I came as soon as I could." By *soon*, I mean I had to drive the speed limit because I had a couple of glasses of wine with Andrew before showing up here, and the last thing I need tonight is trouble with the law.

Susan is bundled up in a scarf and sweater. I can't tell if she's calm or scared, maybe both. I toss my winter coat onto an empty seat.

"So, you found it okay?" she asks.

How could I forget? This is where I brought Ronan last summer when a burdock lodged itself in his throat. I absolutely blew past the speed limit that day, with Ronan hacking in the back seat of my car. I thought he was going to die. He ended up swallowing the burdock, and they sent us on our way with a little doggie Maalox. I drove back home that night feeling like the luckiest girl in the world.

"How is Picabo?"

"They're evaluating her right now."

I had assumed that I'd walk in here, and Susan would be ready to go home, but I think we're in for a long night. Earlier today, Picabo gave birth to six puppies, but an X-ray showed that there were still two more inside.

"Thanks for coming," she says. "Jake is at home with the other puppies."

"Of course. You know how much I love Picabo."

I hope I can stay awake. Andrew and I are usually in bed this time of night, just after Jake takes the dogs out for the last time and turns off the outside light.

"Too bad they don't have a minibar here. Hey, but they have snacks!" I pry open a mini bag of Doritos. I've been eating more than usual lately, but this is how it's always been for me. When I'm happy, I eat too much.

"Susan?"

A vet hurries into the waiting room. Susan stands, kneading the fringe on her scarf with her hands. "What's the latest?"

"One of the puppies doesn't have a heartbeat. The other one does, but I have to tell you, the odds aren't good."

Oh my God. This is terrible. I don't think Susan has ever lost two puppies before, not even when Rooney had a litter of ten.

"Just do what you need to do! Try and save them."

"We'll do our best," the vet says. "We just needed your permission..."

"Yes! Yes! Go!"

If there's one thing Susan hates, it's feeling like she's not in control. There's nothing we can do right now but wait and hope for the best.

"Do you want anything?" I ask, waving my empty bag of Doritos at her. "It's free..."

"Get another Doritos and a bag of Cheetos too. Sorry to ruin your night." She pats an empty chair. "Sit down. Distract me. Tell me what's going on with Andrew."

"He wants me to meet his kids," I say, licking Dorito dust off my fingers.

"That's great! That means he really wants to be official."

"Do you have homes for your puppies? Maybe we should get one. That'll make it official real fast."

"Do you want another puppy?"

I'm half-kidding. I know there's no chance of that happening, not now at least. Susan always has a waitlist. I've been wanting a companion for Ronan for a long time, but I know it would shake things up, the way it did with Jack.

"Maybe a year from now?" Susan says.

"Maybe."

I've always found a reason to wait. I don't have enough money. My apartment is too small. Can I handle the stress of another dog who likes to eat socks, seat belts and soccer balls?

"Would Andrew be up for it?"

"He would. He thinks Ronan is lonely."

"Could you have a puppy with Andrew's work schedule?"

There she goes with her questions again. It reminds me of when she called me on the phone to screen me about Ronan. I did my best to present my marriage as a happy one, but by that point, I was already concerned about my future.

"Dogs are a lot of work, but that doesn't mean I wouldn't do it again." I've enjoyed giving Ronan everything he's ever wanted in life: hikes, treats, KONG chew toys, blowouts, even sexual experiences with other dogs!

"Maybe you should wait a little longer to get a dog," Susan says. "You and Andrew haven't been together long..."

True, but Andrew and I haven't really been playing by the rules, a strategy that has actually worked for us so far.

"Who's getting your puppies?" I ask. "Any young couples whose marriage is on the verge of collapse?"

"You know that first time we talked on the phone, and I asked you all those questions, I knew something wasn't right in your marriage."

I have always wondered about this. What *did* Susan think about Jack and me? I always thought we put on a good show. How would she have given us a puppy otherwise?

"I asked you about kids. You said you weren't sure."

"What was wrong about that? We just got married."

"You hesitated. I could hear the worry in your voice."

All this time, I thought Susan was as surprised as everyone else that my marriage didn't work out, but even so, that doesn't explain one thing. "So why did you give me Ronan then? If you thought my marriage was in trouble?"

"Because I liked you."

Maybe she just had a good feeling, the way I had a hunch about moving to Hanover.

A couple wanders out with a cat meowing in a carrier. Glad Ronan isn't here to see that. He'd go nuts. I glance at my phone. Andrew has stopped texting, so he must be asleep by now, trying to out-snore Ronan. Andrew always ends up sleeping in some weird position because Ronan stretches out onto his back and takes up all the room.

"Susan?"

It's the veterinarian who operated on Picabo. She wipes her forehead and looks at me, then Susan. "Only one of the puppies was alive by the time we could get to them. I'm so sorry. I wish we had been able to save them both."

"I should have come sooner," Susan says.

"You did the best you could with the information you had," I say. "And Picabo is okay, and they saved a puppy."

"Who survived?" Susan asks. "Boy? Girl?"

"Girl," the vet says. "A brindle."

A girl! When Susan and I first talked about her puppies, I was hoping for a girl, but we wound up with Ronan, and now I can't imagine my life turning out any other way.

"Give us a few more minutes to get everyone ready, and then you can all go home," the vet says.

Could I rearrange my bedroom to accommodate a puppy crate? It's February, which means by the time the puppy would be ready to live with us, it would be spring. The perfect time to potty-train. If I want three dogs in my future, maybe it's time to get moving. All I need is a good name for her.

"Maybe it's time for me to get that girl I always wanted."

"Now? Are you sure?"

"You know how much I love Picabo. Why are you hesitating? Don't you think I'm better than that guy from the military who joked about killing us? Don't you want this little girl around all the time? You know I'd make a good puppy parent."

"Betsy, relax. I just think it's funny that we're back here again."

She's right. New guy, new dog. The start of a new story.

"Just don't promise her to someone else, okay? I know you have a waitlist but give me a chance to talk about it with Andrew."

We've polished off another bag of Cheetos by the time the vet returns with Picabo and the smallest puppy I have ever seen. I cannot believe she's still alive.

"She can't see you, but she can smell you," Susan says, handing me the puppy.

The first time I held Ronan in Susan's backyard, he couldn't wait to run off and explore, but this girl is completely different. She's incredibly affectionate. She's going to be absolutely fine with all my smothering. "I love her."

"Well, at least this means I'll have one less puppy person to screen. I know everything about you. Where you live, what you like to eat, the car you drive. I even know what your vibrator looks like. But what happens if it doesn't work out with you and Andrew? Who gets custody?"

Easy answer. "Me."

Susan holds the door as we step out into the night. "Don't worry. If it's too much, you can always return her."

We both know there's no chance in hell of that ever happening. Only one dog has been brought back to Susan's, and it's the same one who started this entire thing. Ronan.

MIGRATION SEASON
(One Year Later)

That's Amore!

"Are we still going to share a *New Yorker* subscription after you move?" Susan asks during a *Jeopardy!* commercial break. Tonight's categories have been excellent: *TV Stars, Biographies & Memoirs, Classic Songs,* and *Ends With A 3-Letter Body Part*, which sounds kind of dirty.

"We're only going to be ten minutes away from you," I say. "That's basically the time span of a *Double Jeopardy!* round."

A couple months from now, Andrew and I are moving to our own home in Vermont.

It's mud season now, but by then, it will be summer. After two and a half years of living in Susan's apartment, I'm ready for a change. It feels like the right time. Andrew's divorce has been finalized, and I'm turning forty in May.

Last winter, Andrew and I started looking at homes for fun. We saw a midcentury modern property in Hanover right around the corner from Susan's. It was the right price but hadn't been on the market in forty-plus years and needed a lot of work. We also looked at a musty log cabin and a home on Lake Sunapee that was out of our price range and too far away from Hanover.

Then in January, we found an old farmhouse in Vermont with three bedrooms and seven acres of land. We loved the wraparound porch, the small pond in the woods, and the cozy structure next to the house that used to be a carpentry workshop.

On the day of the viewing, Andrew and I walked from room to room, dreaming about what color to paint the bedroom and where to put the bed in order to have good feng shui. An empty room on the first floor next to a bedroom was easily the best room in the entire house, with two windows looking out into the woods, western-facing to catch the evening sunset.

"Maybe a bathroom?" I said to Andrew.

Or maybe a nursery. We had recently started trying to have children, but I already knew it wasn't going to be easy, given my age. Only time would tell what the room might become.

"We'll be in touch," Andrew said to the realtor.

We zipped up our coats and walked to the car in the driveway. It was a frosty day, the ground covered in a blanket of snow, but the sun was out. We sat in the car to talk it over, watching songbirds fly back and forth between old cedar trees.

Were we ready to buy a home in Vermont? We certainly looked like Vermonters. Andrew was now sporting a beard, and I was stealing his flannel shirts to wear myself.

"We'll have to get a guy to plow the driveway in the winter ... and we'll need a lawn mower ... I wonder what the taxes are ... and we'll have to do an inspection ..." Andrew said.

"I love it," I said.

"Me too."

"Seven acres, we could have farm animals!" I said. "Maybe we could get a donkey?"

Neither of us knew anything about donkeys, but it was still fun to dream.

"We can't just get one. We have to get two. Donkeys need to be in pairs."

I wasn't sure how Andrew knew about the social habits of donkeys or how serious he was about the whole thing, but I wasn't about to argue. Two donkeys sounded better than one.

"Should we make an offer?" I asked.

"Absolutely!"

Susan was quick to point out that the house had some problems, small ones like a broken oven, and a really big one—a busted septic system that the owner didn't want to pay to fix. Did we really want to deal with a difficult owner? We didn't. But the owner changed his mind when we walked away from the deal, and now we're signing the papers in a couple days.

"What are the horoscopes for the closing?" Susan asks, pulling out her iPad. "I hope Mercury isn't retrograde."

I've trained her well. "I would never sign a contract during Mercury retrograde, but I definitely plan on smudging the hell out of that place to remove any bad spirits before we move in."

A clue pops up on the television.

"Jake, turn up the remote!" Susan yells.

"This Michelle Obama memoir was the bestselling hardcover book of 2018."

"*Becoming*!" Susan yells before I have the chance.

I should have gotten that, but I've been too distracted by Woody, a new addition to Susan's pack of dogs. He's been trying to hump me for the last five minutes. I toss a squeaky toy across the room to try and distract him, but he's only interested in my leg. "Maybe you shouldn't have named him Woody."

Susan shrugs. "What can I say? He has a dick and knows how to use it."

"How can you and Andrew leave the nest now?" Jake asks. "We just got Andrew trained on the snowblower."

As much as I love the sight of Andrew out there snow-blowing, at least we won't have to worry about falling on Susan's driveway after we move. And Andrew and I won't have to fight for closet space. And I won't accidentally find Jake's underwear in the dryer. I won't have to rush to my mailbox to get my *New Yorker* before Susan steals it. And in turn, Susan will never have to deal with the tenant stealing her Shout stain remover from the laundry room to remove Ronan's pee stains from the bedspread. She'll never have to manage a lazy renter who doesn't want to pick up frozen dog poops in below-zero temps.

But that also means we'll be saying good-bye to everything that made family night fun: *Jeopardy!*, potluck dinners, and card games. What will it feel like to live in a house where daily life isn't a competition over who made the best entrée or who won March Madness or who ended the day with the lowest resting heartrate? (Poor Jake never wins the latter because of his pacemaker.)

"Just remember, before you move out, all the dryer balls have to be accounted for," Susan says.

If that's the case, we might as well go out and buy some replacements. Surely, the missing balls will just come off my security deposit like everything else. In my time here, I've been running a tab that includes: scratch marks on Susan's coffee table from Ronan using it as a dog bed; the *Good Boy* couch pillow that has holes in it; and a ripped lamp shade, although I've positioned the torn part against the wall. Maybe Susan won't notice? She already knows about the bite marks on the kitchen chair, thanks to Jackie O., our one-year-old puppy who has been ours ever since the night she almost died at the vet's office.

Despite her affinity for flossing her canines with my shoelaces, Jackie Kennedy Onassis is beloved by all of us. Every morning, I pry open my eyes to a scruffy gray face inches away from mine. She follows me from room to room, wagging her tail and whining for affection, and I'm always more than happy to give it to her.

But by far, the best thing about Jackie is that she keeps Ronan young. It's hard to believe that he's seven years old now, middle aged in dog years. He hasn't lost his spunk, though. He still offers stud services and is able to seal the deal in fifteen minutes or less. He loves when Jackie hides under his favorite club chair, then jumps out at him when he's least expecting it. I can't imagine life without Jackie, though it would be nice at some point if she stopped barking at the vacuum cleaner.

"Has Jackie eaten anything else I need to know about?" Susan asks. "Didn't you say she ate your wedding album?"

"Only the box. And I'm divorced. So what does it really matter? One less thing to pack."

A timer goes off in the kitchen. "Tea time!" Susan yells.

Tonight, we're having chamomile. Jake shuffles into the kitchen to check on the teapot. We consume less booze now because we're feeling the effects of aging and trying to be healthier. Susan pressured me for months to drink pu-erh tea to lower my cholesterol. I resisted at first, but once I started drinking it, my numbers actually came down.

"Do you need landscaping done for your house?" Susan asks. "Go to E.C. Brown's, and ask for John. Tell him I sent you. I did his divorce. Do you know your new neighbors yet?"

I don't, but Susan and Jake probably do. They raised their kids in Vermont and keep up with all of the small-town drama on the daily listserv.

"Don't worry," she says. "I started Googling them for you."

I can't believe I ever worried about losing touch with Susan after we move. She's going to be hands-on big time. Every day, she fills our group chat with ideas for paint colors, couches, bed frames, bathtubs, you name it.

"If there's any other furniture you want to make an offer on, we're all ears," Jake says.

What's left? We bought their firepit, a wooden bench to put on our front porch, a small cabinet that was in their laundry room, and a blue abstract painting that always reminded me of a whale's tail and would be perfect in our new bedroom. "The first piece of art I ever bought for myself," Susan once said. We're even taking their loveseat and the mattress from our bed that Susan and Jake made their kids on. Gross if you think about it, but it's actually really comfortable.

"What about the treat jar?" I ask. "Can we take that?"

The dogs would be devasted without it. It's been in my apartment ever since I moved here. I think Susan won it at a dog show. It has a ceramic handle shaped like a Glen terrier, and the lid makes a joyful rattling noise when I take it off. The dogs come running, no matter where they are. I love when Jake stops by to let our dogs out and tells us that the jar is "runnin' on empty" and needs a refill.

"Take anything you want," Jake says. "We're downsizing."

"Well, since it looks like you guys are really moving, I guess we should start looking for a new tenant for our *garden* apartment," Susan says.

"How are you going to advertise the running of the dogs?" Andrew asks, laughing.

That's a great question. Will they tell the tenant beforehand? Or surprise them the way they did with me?

I nearly had a heart attack during that first wakeup call. The dogs' nails scratching Susan's hardwood floors, Rooney running up the hill to chase away the deer, and Ronan barking furiously at the ceiling, wondering what in the hell was going on up there.

"I guess we could say it's a little noisy," Susan says. "Is it really that loud?"

"You should listen to it one of these days," Andrew says. "It sounds like Santa's reindeer up there."

Though it will feel amazing to sleep in past 6 a.m. for once, I have to say that it was the best alarm clock I ever had. It takes a special type of person to appreciate life here. I never thought I would be that person, nor Andrew for that matter. Every fear I had about Andrew fitting in was put to rest the night I came home from a yoga class and found him upstairs sharing a meal with Susan and Jake at the dinner table. Susan had even gone to the trouble of lighting her battery-operated candles, a true sign of a special occasion.

"You guys are eating together? Without me?" I asked.

Andrew shrugged. "I was waiting downstairs for you to come home, but then I heard them playing *Jeopardy!*, so . . ."

I know that's what he loves most about living in this house. As for me, I will miss the dogs fighting for a spot next to me on the couch, even if that means I end up with ripped leggings. Every hole is a sign of love. I will miss Jake coming downstairs to fix the furnace or the shower drain or to properly relocate a lost spider that found its way into my bathtub. Above all, I will miss our upstairs bodega. If we need sour cream for our enchiladas from now on, I guess we'll have to go to the store like normal people instead of borrowing it from Susan.

I had no idea what to expect when Andrew moved in here with us, but this last year has turned out to be one of the best years of my life. Looking back now, I can't believe I ever thought we'd have separate lives. I still remember the day I moved into Susan's house and she pointed out the door that she had installed at the bottom of the circular staircase.

"So you can have some privacy," she explained. "You'll have your world, and we'll have ours."

I wasn't really looking for solitude. I wanted companionship. I had already spent so much of the last year alone. And then, a couple weeks later, Ronan did me a favor. He clawed the door open and got out.

I was mortified. I didn't know Susan and Jake all that well. Would she kick us out if Ronan kept misbehaving? We had nowhere else to go. But to my surprise, she didn't seem to mind him breaking her door all that much.

"I guess he really wanted to get upstairs," she said, laughing.

Soon after that, I was the one going upstairs for *Jeopardy!* and snacks. And soon, the four of us will be doing dinner at our house in Vermont instead of theirs.

At some point, we'll have to start planning for the long-term. What happens a decade from now when Susan and Jake are in their seventies and eighties?

"Don't worry, we'll take care of them," Andrew said to me not that long ago.

Maybe Andrew and I will put a tiny house on our property for Susan and Jake. Maybe we'll go in on a fixer-upper in Italy or a beach house on the Cape that has room for seven dogs. Maybe next time, Andrew and I will be the ones who get to live upstairs.

A clue flashes across the screen.

When the moon hits your eye like a big pizza pie, that's...this.

"Amore!" we yell.

I think for the first-time ever, we all got it right.

*

In the years to come, I'll honk my horn when I drive past Susan's. Sometimes, I'll stop in for tea. Other times, I'll slow down and look through the big kitchen window to see what Susan and Jake are up to. I love seeing them share a meal, the dogs running up and down the hill in the backyard. It reminds me of that really weird time in my life when I moved into a stranger's home and somehow ended up with everything I needed. It reminds me that life sometimes has a plan that's better than the one you had in mind. And that sometimes all you need to do is follow your dog home to get there.

Acknowledgments

As a journalist, I've spent most of my life telling other people's stories. I was in my mid-thirties when the desire to tell my own story caused me to abandon everything for a new life where I could prioritize my writing. It felt like a crazy decision at the time, but in hindsight, it made a lot of sense. This book is the product of a chance I took on myself.

This memoir would not be here without Joni Cole, my friend and writer/editor extraordinaire who has a gift for spotting wisdom on the page. Thank you for guiding me on every step of my journey, for supporting me when I doubted myself, and for helping me find my way, on the page and in life.

To that end, I would like to thank The Writer's Center of White River Junction, Vermont, and my Thursday night writing group who listened to early drafts of this memoir: April, Sasha, Janna, Linda, Tim, Drew, Casey. I was so intimidated to read my words aloud; your laughter and tears and encouragement meant the world to me. I heard everything you said. Thank you to my early readers: Aine, Maeve, Katie.

To Susan and Jake, my friends who have supported me as if they were my own parents. I can be myself with you. What greater gift is there? Thank you for taking care of me in every sense of the word, with food, advice, laughter, and love. This book is for you. Thank you for letting a lost writer into your home. If you don't want your puppy people living with you in the future, maybe you should change your screening process.

To Andrew, my favorite Gemini. Thank you for being the type of person who brings me a refill on my coffee while I'm doing my morning pages. This book exists because of your love and encouragement. I treasure our life with the dogs, even if it means our bed is sometimes too crowded. I wouldn't have it any other way.

To my father, to Pean, to my publisher. Thank you. Also, my utmost thanks to Wendy Willis Baldwin, Kelly McMasters, Ernest Scheyder, and Marjorie Matthews.

Thank you to my spiritual coven. To my astrologer, Leslie Galbraith, for teaching me the language of the stars. To Colleen McCann, who supplied the perfect crystal concoction to get me through the revision process. To Kim Krans for inventing her magical Spirit Animal deck. To Magic Jewelry for my black cloud aura photo. To the witches at Enchantments and Magic Hour who crafted my magical candles. Guess what? They worked.

About the Author

Betsy Vereckey lives in Norwich, Vermont. She started her career as a journalist with the Associated Press in Athens, Greece, and has been publishing professionally for over twenty years. Her personal essays have appeared in the *Los Angeles Times*, the *Washington Post*, the *Boston Globe* and *Food & Wine* magazine. Her story about asking a baker out on a date was featured in *The New York Times'* Modern Love column, and one of her personal essays about her recipe for divorce potatoes was the third most popular food story in the *Washington Post* the year it appeared.

She earned a degree in psychology from American University and a master's degree in journalism from Ohio University on a full scholarship. Betsy is married to the love interest in her memoir. They have three Glen of Imaal terriers and live in an old farmhouse that was dragged down the street to its current location by oxen over a century ago. She is also a practicing astrologer and volunteers at the Vermont Institute of Natural Science with injured raptors and baby songbirds.

Visit her website, www.betsyvereckey.com, to learn more.

🌿We Grow Our Books in Montpelier, Vermont

Learn more about our titles in Fiction, Nonfiction, Poetry and Children's Literature at the QR code below or visit www.rootstockpublishing.com.

www.ingramcontent.com/pod-product-compliance
Lightning Source LLC
Chambersburg PA
CBHW030516080526
44586CB00011B/214